Patrick Chukwudezie Chibuko

C0-ALX-271

# Keeping the Liturgy Alive

Patrick Chukwudezie Chibuko

# Keeping the Liturgy Alive

## An Anglophone West African Experience

IKO – Verlag für Interkulturelle Kommunikation

BX
1977
.A35
C452
2003

Bibliographische Information der Deutschen Bibliothek
Die Deutsche Bibliothek verzeichnet diese Publikation in der Deutschen Nationalbibliographie; detaillierte bibliographische Daten sind im Internet über http://dnb.ddb.de abrufbar.

© IKO-Verlag für Interkulturelle Kommunikation
Frankfurt am Main • London, 2003

Frankfurt am Main          London
Postfach 90 04 21          70 c, Wrentham Avenue
D - 60444 Frankfurt       London NW10 3HG, UK

e-mail: info@iko-verlag.de • Internet: www.iko-verlag.de

ISBN: 3-88939-704-5

Umschlaggestaltung:     Volker Loschek, 61184 Karben
Herstellung:            DVS Digitaler Vervielfältigungs- und VerlagsService,
                        60325 Frankfurt a. M.

Distribution for
North America, South America, Asia, Australia, New Zealand and Africa by

Transaction Publishers,
Rutgers, The State University,
35 Berrue Circle, Piscataway,
New Jersey 08854
United States of America

# DEDICATION

To all the Ex-alumni of Pontifical Institute of Liturgy (PIL) Rome,
Home Branch, Nigeria.

# TABLE OF CONTENTS

# ACKNOWLEDGEMENTS

For the wisdom, strength and inspiration I remain ever indebted to God the Father of our Lord Jesus Christ in the unity of the Holy Spirit.

For correcting the scripts to make it eligible, I owe a lot of thanks to my closest colleagues and friends: Rev. Fr. Lawrence Madubuko who not only read the work critically and recommended it, he also wrote the Foreword. Rev. Fr. Augustine Oburota must be greatly appreciated for taking the pains to improve the quality of this work. In a very outstanding manner, I express my profound gratitude to all those who rendered help at any stage of this work. In addition to my collective thanks to you, I wish you all, God's choicest blessings now and in the years ahead.

Patrick Chukwudezie Chibuko.
Holy Trinity Sunday,
15th June, 2003.

# GENERAL LIST OF ABBREVIATIONS

| | |
|---|---|
| AAS | *Acta Apostolicae Sedis*, Vaticanis, 1909 -. |
| CCC | Catechism of the Catholic Church. |
| CMRR | Ceremonies of the Modern Roman Rite, 1995. |
| Col. | Colossians. |
| Cor. | Corinthians. |
| DV | *Dei Verbum* (Dogmatic Constitution on Divine Revelation) 1965. |
| Eccl. | Ecclesiasticus. |
| Eph. | Ephesians. |
| Ex. | Exodus. |
| Gen. | Genesis. |
| Heb. | Hebrews. |
| IGRM | *Institutio Generalis Missalis Romani*, 2000. |
| Ibid. | *Ibidem.* |
| Is. | Isaiah. |
| Jer. | Jeremiah. |
| Jn. | John. |
| Lk. | Luke. |
| LG. | *Lumen Gentium* (Dogmatic Constitution on the Church) 1972. |
| Mk. | Mark. |
| Matt. | Matthew. |
| Op. cit. | *Opus citatus.* |
| PG. | *Patrologiae Cursus Completus, Series Graeca,* Migne J. P. ed., Paris. |
| PL. | *Patrologiae Cursus Completus, Series Latina,* Migne J. P. ed., Paris. |
| Ps. | Psalm. |
| PO. | *Presbyterorum Ordinis* (Decree on the Ministry and Life of Priests) 1965. |

| | |
|---|---|
| RGIRM. | Revised General Instruction on the Roman Missal, 2000. |
| Rom. | Romans. |
| SC. | *Sacrosanctum Concilium* (The Constitution on the Sacred Liturgy) 1963. |

# FOREWORD

For anyone alert to the liturgical literature in West African sub-region Fr. Patrick Chukwudezie Chibuko needs no introduction. Fr. Chibuko was the pioneer holder of the seat of Sacred Liturgy in the Catholic Institute of West Africa, Port Harcourt, River State, Nigeria (1991-2001). He has written a good number of books including the *Igbo Christian Rite of Marriage*; *Paschal Mystery of Christ: Foundation for Liturgical Inculturation in Africa and Liturgical Inculturation: An Authentic African Response*. He has also to his credit numerous articles published in learned journals and published monographs including *Traditional Marriage and Church Wedding in one Ceremony*.

In his present work, **Keeping The Liturgy Alive: An Anglophone West African Experience**, he has presented a passionate case for the rehabilitation of Liturgy in the Church within the West African sub-region. Such a rehabilitation goes beyond mere lip service to the great importance of liturgy in the life of the Church. indeed, in the vision of the Fathers of the Second Vatican Council, healthy spirituality as well as adequate Ecclesiology are both dependent on authentic liturgy. Rightly therefore, does the author call for serious attention to liturgy from the formative years and in the intellectual formation of liturgical actors notably priests, religious and some members of the laity.

In **Keeping The Liturgy Alive**, Fr. Chibuko has focused on a number of themes which can rightly now be described as his trade mark - his insistence on Paschal Mystery and his call for a sense of awe in liturgy. He has also directed our attention to more practical issues like the homily and the maintenance of healthy balance in actual celebration.

Having been a major actor in the just concluded Third National Eucharistic Congress in Ibadan, Nigeria (November 15-17, 2002), it would have been a surprise if such a huge liturgical experience had not impinged on the author. Indeed, it appears that the experience was the immediate background of his writing for he climaxed and concluded his writing with a tentative inculturated model of a Mass for a Eucharistic Congress.

Various readers will drop *Keeping The Liturgy Alive* with their respective opinions about its merit as a whole and in parts. For instance whereas some readers may question the justification of the proposed Mass formulary the present writer finds rewarding the focus on homily and on the issue of balance.

Perhaps the indisputable fact about *Keeping The Liturgy Alive* is that it represents for the Church in West Africa the liturgical agenda and that on the two fronts of pastoral action and academic enquiry and even at that alone Fr. Chibuko has done us a veritable public service – a liturgy in the original sense of it.

Lawrence Madubuko (Rev. Fr.)
Department of Liturgy
Blessed Iwene Tansi Major Seminary, Onitsha.
11.01.03.

# KEEPING THE LITURGY ALIVE

## AN ANGLO-PHONE WEST AFRICAN EXPERIENCE

### GENERAL INTRODUCTION

Keeping the liturgy alive sets out to review the status of liturgy in the An-glo-phone West African sub-region. Could the church in the sub-region be said to have really taken liturgy serious and given it the rightful status it deserves in the scheme of things? To what extent is the church in the sub-region responding effectively to the demands of the liturgical reforms of the Second Vatican Council? The Council Fathers made series of calls to-wards the optimal development of the liturgy both as science and praxis. With regard to trained liturgists, the document on the sacred liturgy, *Sacro-sanctum Concilium* says: Professors who are appointed to teach liturgy in seminaries, religious houses of studies, and theological faculties, must be properly trained for their work in institutes which specialise in this subject.[1]

One may rightly ask, what is the situation today regarding the status of the Liturgy in the sub-region? Those who are appointed to teach liturgy in the major seminaries and theological faculties and Institutes, are they qualified? Have they studied in institutes specialised in this subject? Are they numerically enough to handle the demanding needs in the major semi-naries and religious institutes? What about the liturgy in the dioceses? Within the sub-region what specialised institutes are there on ground where liturgy could well be taught and studied at various levels? The document further says that: the study of Sacred Liturgy is to be ranked among the compulsory and major courses in seminaries and religious houses of stud-ies. In theological faculties it is to rank among the principal courses. It is to be taught under its theological, historical, spiritual, pastoral, and juridical aspects (I add with a view to inculturation). In addition, those who teach other subjects, especially dogmatic theology, sacred scripture, spiritual and pastoral theology, should, each of them submitting to the exigencies of his own discipline, expounding the mystery of Christ and the history of salvation in a manner that will clearly set forth the connection between their subjects and the liturgy, and the unity which underlines all priestly training.[2]

What is the status of liturgical studies in the major seminaries today, theological Faculties and Institutes? Is liturgy treated as it should be, as a *compulsory, major* course? Is it among the principal courses? What is its status vis-à-vis *other compulsory, major and principal courses?* Do the authorities respect the laudable mentality of the Africans, who attach great importance and value to what one has seriously laboured for, shown in the high marks scored with a certificate to back it up as a tangible evidence? Presently, liturgy as a course does not seem to be offered in the first theological degree examination (Bachelor of Divinity). One could discern a lurking tendency towards marginalisation and lack of seriousness towards the very thing that is being considered as the life-wire of the church beginning right from the place of formation. Since it is not offered in the first theological degree (BD), the tendency could be for the staff and students to take it easy (when it cannot be taken easy any more, but seriously). If it is the melting point of all theological studies, it should appear as a degree material in the BD.

In the existing theological faculties and Institutes within the sub-region, what is obtainable as regards liturgical science and praxes? As an exclusive Institute for theological scientific research and inculturation, in what form does liturgy exist? Is it having the status it deserves as demanded by the Second Vatican Council, or is it just receiving a lip service? Does liturgy vie effectively with other theological courses in readiness to respond to the myriad of liturgical issues of the moment especially liturgical inculturation? A theological faculty without at least a department of Sacred Liturgy is to say the least incomplete and absolutely missing the mark. Theology remains dead until it is celebrated in the liturgy. Theology dwells in the realm of theory until liturgy down-loads and packages it into practical worshipping forms. For among the major components of theology is the sacred liturgy. No wonder then the Fathers of the Second Vatican Council considered liturgy as a primary point in the entire reformation of the life of the church.

What one often seems to forget is that, in the life of the church, the only place where intelligence, excellent knowledge of other theological disciplines are best manifested before all else is in the liturgical celebration. If the liturgy is so important in the life of the church what then could be responsible for the lack of seriousness which is very evident especially in the sub-region?

In the same vein, ignorance compels some others to think of liturgy as playing guitars and having joyful pieces of noise, of exuberance, movement, banners and enthusiastic congregations. Some others think of liturgy in terms of strict adherence to rubrics. For them rubricism defines liturgy. As a consequence of ignorance, some think of liturgy in terms of gathering of friends and neighbours in someone's home for a careful reading of the Scriptures, for spontaneous prayer, and for intimate sharing of the one bread and the one cup. Some still think of it in terms of solemn ritual and beautiful music, a liturgy of pomp and circumstance, speaking of concern to put the best of human gifts and talents at the service of worshipping the transcendent God. [3]

Today all over the world, there is a clarion call, to indigenise, contextualise, inculturate the liturgy according to cultural values and the genius of the people. Certainly the present marginalising tendency with the very low status given to liturgy in the seminaries, in the higher theological faculties, institutes and religious houses do not augur well for the future of liturgy.

Liturgists are often confronted with the nagging question: *give us a new liturgy that is truly christian and fully cultural*. The present state of apparent marginalisation of the liturgy and mass ignorance of the subject cannot answer that question effectively. It means either that those demanding an inculturated liturgy do not mean what they are asking for or they are not serious in their demand for inculturation or they are not even sure of what they are asking for. Liturgy requires a much better enabling environment to be able to address squarely the numerous liturgical questions facing the church today.

Inculturation demands more than mere asking. It does more with doing. It is not merely discussion but a matter of decision and commitment. It is not a haphazard affair. It requires a faculty or at least a department within a tertiary academic set up where scientific study and systematic praxes could well take place under the close supervision of liturgical experts. Liturgy to remain alive, requires a favourable academic atmosphere where experts could converge and rub minds together in order to evolve befitting and practical rites that are essentially christian and fully cultural. Liturgical inculturation like every aspect of theology that demands inculturation, requires a well thought out, systematic study of the liturgy as a science with methodology and clear objectives and the scientific study of the culture of a people to be able to evolve an authentic inculturated liturgy that brings about genuine liturgical praxes which will be homely to the people.

Liturgical inculturation goes beyond the present practice of translation of the official liturgical books from Rome, which serve only as typical editions (*editio typica*) which are open to adaptation or preferably to inculturation. Every translation carries a certain degree of betrayal. In effect, they exist as mere format on the universal level to assist local churches in evolving an authentic, creative, innovative and original rite that reflects the sentiments, the values and genius of a given people. To remain at the level of merely translating those typical editions into local languages is minimal with regard to the enormous tasks demanded by inculturation.

It is equally strange to qualify as inculturation by merely adjusting the structure of already existing rite like the order of Mass, or by haphazardly introducing elements which are obnoxious to the spirit of the liturgy, all in the name of inculturation. Liturgical inculturation requires experts equipped with the good knowledge of the principles of the liturgy, possessing proper tools and facilities, scholarship, libraries and professors in the field. Otherwise one could be scratching only the surface of inculturation and not doing any serious job in this regard.

In the pages of this book, efforts are being made through the chapters to see how much could be done to keep the liturgy alive. First by examining the notion of liturgy both as a theological science with aims, objectives and methodology and practical liturgy as it is celebrated with life.

We made practical proposals towards an area in liturgy that is often glossed over namely the nature of liturgical edifice especially a church building with all that should go with an ideal one in a given time and locality. In the third chapter, serious attempt has been made towards evolving an inculturated local rite of eucharistic celebration enriched with the cultural values and the genius of the people.

The fourth chapter discusses the role of announcements and extra collections. These should be given their rightful place in the liturgy so that they do not constitute an organised distraction which overburden the eucharistic celebration, thus killing the spirit of the celebration instead of keeping the liturgy alive. The fifth chapter treats evangelisation as an indispensable and essential duty of the church. Through evangelisation Christ diffuses himself to all cultures and people. Liturgy in no small measure is seen as the source of nourishment in the work of evangelisation. Through the process of evangelisation, sacred liturgy is kept very much alive.

Chapter six deals with enriched liturgical gestures and postures which are considered to be favourable means of keeping liturgy alive. The seventh chapter handles liturgical homily in a very broad and objective manner. Liturgical homily which draws from the texts of the celebration is considered to be a first class nourishment for the life of the church. The Word of God powerfully proclaimed, skilfully commented upon and aptly applied surely edifies the church, namely the people of God.

Finally, the book discusses extensively what it considers as abuses, aberrations, anomalies and exaggerations that could run down the integrity of the liturgy if not timely checked. The ultimate invitation lies in the acceptance of and faithful observance of the instructions as contained in the New Roman Missal of the third Millennium or as contained in the Revised General Instruction on the Roman Missal of July, 2000.

The appendices contain practical liturgical compositions. The first deals with a collective response of a nation united to celebrate their national unity within the context of Eucharistic Congress. It has interjectory response in the entire eucharistic prayer. The second varies from the first because the interjections appear only at consecration. The rationale behind this is to recall the need for an enhance active participation in the liturgy. It goes further to underscore the African way of interjectory response in their praying form.

# CHAPTER ONE
# NOTION OF THE LITURGY

## Introduction

To undertake a meaningful reform and renewal of the life of the church, the Fathers of the Second Vatican Council began with the reformation of the church's liturgy. This goes to underscore the eminent position of the liturgy in the life of the church. The vitality of any church can well be measured by the vibrant nature of her worshipping form. The liturgy is seen as the life-wire of the church; her nerve-centre. It is the very life of the church. A church without the liturgy could well be considered a dead church. Just as the uncelebrated Word of God could well be considered as a dead Word of God. The church becomes meaningful, alive, dynamic, relevant and vibrant when she celebrates her liturgy. Another way of saying that the liturgy facilitates the salvific mission of the church. The liturgy makes the church really alive. The church one must recall is Christ and members. The members include the clergy, the religious and the laity. Whatever applies to the church applies as well to all the members and vice versa.

## The Nature of Liturgy

We shall consider liturgy as the celebration of the Paschal Mystery of Christ. This is the mystery through which Christ accomplished the work of human salvation.[4] It is this mystery of Christ that the church proclaims and celebrates in her liturgy so that the faithful may live from it and bear witness to it in the world.[5] Following the finest definition of Pope Pius X11, liturgy means that public worship which our redeemer as head of the church renders to the Father, as well as the worship which the community of the faithful renders to its Founder, and through him to the heavenly Father. Briefly speaking, it means that public worship rendered by the Mystical Body of Christ in the entirety of its head and members.[6] This is also the sense in which the reformed liturgy of the Second Vatican Council conceived the liturgy of the church.[7] The liturgy is well understood as that celebration which renders Christ present for the transformation unto sanctification of the members, the edification of the church and the glorification of God through authentic witnessing. Before then, the Council has outlined the various ways in which Christ is present in the liturgy in order to be able to effect the above mentioned results as follows:

a) Christ is present in the worshipping assembly *for where two or three are gathered in my name, there am I in their midst* (Matt. 18:20).

b) Christ is present in the proclaimed Word. For when the Word is proclaimed it is Christ proclaiming Himself to the assembly through the agency of the lector. In other words, he is both the proclaimed and the one proclaiming.[8]

c) Christ is present in the sacraments that are being celebrated. Such that when anybody baptises it is really Christ himself who baptises.

d) Christ is present in the minister as he performs the ministry of his vocation.

e) Christ is present in the Eucharist *(par excellence)* in a most excellent manner.[9] In the Eucharist, Christ adheres strictly to the species of bread and wine as his body and blood and this presence remains permanently during and after consecration and continues to remain present as long as the nature of bread still remains intact.

Liturgy is essentially Trinitarian. The three Persons of the Blessed Trinity form the basis in the celebration of the mystery of salvation. The church's liturgy is patterned to be addressed to the Father, through the Son in the unity of the Holy Spirit; *ad Patrem, per Filium in Sancto Spiritu.*[10] In the liturgy, all christian prayer finds its source and goal.

Liturgy is rightly considered as the *culmen et fons* of the activities of the church. It remains that summit towards which all the activities of the church is directed; and at the same time, the fount from which all the church's power flow.[11] It is the source from which the church draws its powers. It could further be explained as that ecclesial action *par excellence* as well as the unique source for theology and vice versa < *liturgy=locus theologicus; theology=locus liturgicus*>.

It needs also to be noted, that the liturgy does not exhaust the entire activity of the church.[12] Against this background, the Catechism of the Catholic Church further explains that the liturgy must be preceded by evangelisation, faith and conversion. It can then produce ist fruits in the lives of the faithful: new life in the spirit and, involvement in the mission of the church and service to her unity.[13]

From the liturgy one discovers, the faith, the morals, the doctrine and way of life of the church reduced in the common parlance as: *lex orandi – lex credendi – lex vivendi – lex operandi*. In other words, tell me how you worship and I will tell you what you believe in, your morality, your way of life.

It was Pope Pius X1, who taught that the liturgy is the most important organ of the ordinary *magisterium* of the church. The liturgy is not the *Didascalia* of this or that individual doctrine, but the *Didascalia* of the church.

Liturgy encompasses far more than texts and statements, instead it is the expression of a church actively living, praising God and bringing about a holy communion with God through Christ. Thus it has to be respected as a communal event which discloses and articulates the action of God in mystery.

Liturgy is fundamentally eschatological and doxological. One only speaks about God, when one speaks with God; hence theologians need to be attentive to this doxological aspect when drawing theological implications from the liturgy. This is so because, as said earlier, liturgy models one towards transformation into Christ and continual formation in the Christian life.

As a privileged act of the praying church, the texts and actions that comprise the liturgy form a most central source for developing a theology that describes what occurs in liturgy. Liturgy arouses the act of faith in the believer, not merely instructions about acts of faith. The chief aim of the liturgy as an act of the body of Christ, is to engage the community in an act of prayer. In a very broad sense, the liturgy exceeds the celebration of the divine worship to include also, the proclamation of the Gospel and active charity.[14]

## Liturgy among other theological Sciences

Most liturgical historians and experts regard liturgy as *locus theologicus*. They conceive liturgy as a unique source for theology. While others see theology as *locus liturgicus*, that means making theology as a unique source for liturgy. The development of the argument raises some degree of curiosity. What really makes the liturgy a unique source for theology is that it is a ritual event and therefore clearly distinguished from other theological sources, such as statements of the magisterium. Consequently, it is essential to employ a hermeneutic that respects the event character of liturgy especially, liturgical language and liturgical action.[15] It is then worthy of note that the uniqueness of the liturgy as the action of the church that mediates the community's experience of God.[16]

The uniqueness of liturgy lies in the fact that it is the action of the church which mediates the community's experience of God. Thus as a theological source, the liturgy cannot be used as an arsenal of arguments for apologetic purposes. Instead it serves as the privileged teaching (*didascalia*) of the church. It makes use of the fullness of the Christian mystery and is the means through which the church continually experiences the paschal mystery.[17]

I. H. Dalmais however, in his influential monograph, *Initiation a la Liturgie*, gives priority to the liturgy as an ecclesial event rather than to its didactic or informational character. He insists that while sacramental theology deals with what God does for the church in acts of salvation, liturgy deals with the action of the church as it performs acts of worship.[18] While linking liturgy with the deposit of faith, he maintained that the liturgy is the church's permanent catechesis because its proper function is to bring alive the mystery of salvation. The liturgy indeed is the privileged place for catechising the people of God. Catechesis is intrinsically linked with the whole of liturgical and sacramental activity, for it is in the sacraments especially in the Eucharist, that Christ Jesus works in fullness for the transformation of God's people.[19] One must therefore be attentive to the total liturgical action. Each element, text, or rite needs to be interpreted in relation to the other parts of the liturgy.[20]

Liturgy centres on key moments in salvation history and one's contemporary experience of them. Theology is the church's reflection on the work of the church in liturgy. He further maintained that one must be attentive to the total liturgical action. These invariably explain how the law of prayer establishes the law of belief – *lex celebrandi – lex credendi* and *Liturgy as locus theologicus*.

In another development, he believes that the liturgy is fundamentally eschatological and doxological. This incidentally is an important aspect of the liturgy that seems to be glossed over by both liturgists and theologian. An awareness such as this, in turn should make them appreciate the place of doxological language in theology itself.[21] Secondly, liturgy orients the church towards transformation into Christ and continual formation in the christian life. Therefore, liturgy cannot be placed on a par with other theological sciences. For as the privileged act of the praying church – *ecclesia orans*, the texts and the actions that comprise the liturgy form a most central source for developing a theology that describes what occurs in liturgy.

A famous Italian liturgist, Cipriano Vagaggini, underscores yet another important dimension of the liturgy. He maintains that a proper interpretation requires that one respects the varied literary genres within the liturgy and that the main purpose of liturgy is to enact the mystery of faith.[22] The teaching function in the liturgy concerns arousing an act of faith in the believer, not instructing about acts of faith. The chief aim of the liturgy as an act of the body of Christ, is to engage the community in an act of prayer. He invariably insists that theological exploration begins and ends with engaging in the liturgy itself.[23]

For Salvatore Marsili, another interesting Italian liturgist, liturgy is theology par excellence with two basic components. First it is biblical theology in the sense that the word is revealed in every act of liturgy. Second it is fundamentally a liturgical theology because the revealed word is enacted and operative among the faith community at worship. Marsili's work is Christologically rich and ecclesiologically grounded, insofar as he profoundly articulates the uniqueness of Christ's saving paschal mystery while stressing that Christ's followers experience this divine work again and again in worship.[24]

Marsili believes that a theology of liturgy must necessarily include Christology, ecclesiology and pneumatology as well as respect one's present corporate experience of the paschal mystery.[25] He links Scripture with the liturgy by stating that just as Scripture in all its parts is always the announcement of salvation, so the liturgy in all its moments is always the fulfilment of salvation in ritual.[26] He insists that the sacramentality of revelation, and Christ as sacrament containing the totality of revelation, the economy of salvation is realised through the liturgy, the paschal mystery of Christ and the attentiveness to the word of God is actualised through the act of liturgy.[27]

Gerard Lukken in a most thrilling contribution holds that the liturgy is both *theologia* and *orthodoxia prima*. According to him, in the early church and especially in the East, the liturgy was known as *theologia prima* – first theology and dogmatic speculation as *theologia secunda* – second theology. The first meaning of orthodoxy was *right praise (ortho – doxia)* in the liturgy and it is only in the secondary derived sense that it came to mean right teaching. It is therefore, quite legitimate to speak of an *orthodoxia prima* and an *orthodoxia secunda*.[28]

He further maintains that the liturgy is quite properly the first source and norm of faith from which teaching is derived. Since the liturgy is the church's self expression through a complex of words and symbols, the liturgical expression of faith is much richer than any intellectual expression or justification of faith in theological argument or dogmatic pronouncement.

He establishes a very practical balance of mutual relationship between liturgy and dogma. He acknowledges that *theologica secunda* can and should stand as an important corrective to the liturgy, without which the Spirit is always in danger of being extinguished in the liturgy. He opines a relationship of constant dialogue between *theologia* and *orthodoxia prima* and *secunda* which is essential if one is to ensure that the liturgy does not become isolated from the faith of the church and that the faith of the church does not become sterile and moribund.

In his own opinion, Alexander Schmemann holds that without liturgical theology, our understanding of the church's faith and doctrine is bound to be incomplete. The purpose of liturgy is to constitute the church, whose foremost expression is the church at Eucharist. It is not the church which exists for the cult, but the cult for the church, for her welfare, for her growth into the full measure of the stature of Christ. Schmemann is very much convinced that the liturgy not only has an abstract theological meaning but it also is the living norm of theology; it is in the liturgy that the sources of faith, the Bible or Scripture and tradition become a living reality.[29]

It was Aidan Kavanagh who asserted the primacy of worship over belief – *orandi* over *credendi*. He systematically argues that the *statuat* in *legem credendi lex stataut supplicandi* does not allow for these two to be understood as equal. Secondly, he does not believe that the abbreviation *lex orandi, lex credendi* captures the original meaning of the idiom. While admitting that belief does shape worship, he emphasises that worship founds or constitutes belief. The liturgy is primarily an act as opposed to a theory or a creed. As a ritual, liturgy is primarily to be done not studied.[30] Kavanagh further maintains that hearing the Scriptures in the worshipping assembly and acknowledging their anamnetic nature and purpose precedes any theological reflection of a specifically doctrinal sort. True pastoral theology involves worship and living sustained by the word of God.[31]

Several other authors abound who believe in the unique place of the liturgy in the life of the church. The experts whose brilliant views we have presented speak volumes on the primacy of the liturgy in the scheme of things relating to the sustenance of the spiritual life of the church. The liturgy both as public worship and liturgical theology which is the scientific study of liturgy like every branch of theology cannot be over emphasised.


## Prominence of Liturgy Among Other Theological Sciences

The document on the Sacred Liturgy of the Second Vatican Council, SC. 16 states that the study of sacred liturgy is to be ranked among the compulsory and major courses in seminaries and religious houses of studies. In theological faculties it is to rank among the principal courses. It is to be taught under its theological, historical, spiritual, pastoral and juridical aspects (with a view to inculturation). In addition, those who teach other subjects, especially dogmatic theology, sacred scripture, spiritual and pastoral theology, should – each of them submitting to the exigencies of his own discipline – expounding the mystery of Christ and the history of salvation in a manner that will clearly set forth the connection between their subjects and the liturgy, and the unity which underlines all priestly training.

How could one access the status of liturgical studies in major seminaries and theological faculties today? Is it really having the kind of importance and relationship with other courses as demanded? What is its relationship with other compulsory, major and principal courses?

These contributions are certainly enormous and they ought to generate great interest in the liturgy. Liturgy remains the unique locus where the vitality of the church could well be measured. As such every aspect of it has to be well looked into both theory and practice. To maintain its prominent position in the life of the church, it demands a concerted effort at all levels by all especially those at the highest level of every local church's administration.

When the church says that the liturgy does not exhaust the entire activity of the church, it tends to delimit the scope of liturgy. The same applies in determining the notion of the liturgy. It simply goes to underscore the conspicuous or the distinguishing character of liturgy in relation to other theological sciences. One does expect that the theological sciences should have a mutual relationship with the liturgy both in theory and in practice.

Second there appears no clear cut demarcation between liturgical theology and liturgical celebration. Liturgical theology is not the end product of general theological reflections on liturgy. It is neither the case whereby those theological reflections go to give meaning to those liturgical celebrations nor liturgy shaping and strengthening one's theological reflections. Rather the situation exists whereby the very celebration of the liturgy shows even the rich theology embedded in it. This incidentally has been the plight of many theologians and liturgists hitherto especially in the West African Sub-region, a predicament which this work respectfully addresses.

## Practical Liturgy in Question Today

An essential aspect of practical liturgy is aesthetics. Aesthetic dimension of the liturgy deals in essence with practical principles relating to the beauty, taste and arts. Many things are hereby included. It involves specific liturgical law, which for instance directly embraces the rule of celebration, affecting the actions, words, songs, ritual acts, and the circumstances or environment: churches and baptisteries, furnishings, vesture etc.

It includes furthermore, new styles, new spirit in liturgical law. Specifically this affects language, song, and other musical forms, ritual gestures and actions, and material objects of every kind. On the other hand, it may be easy to state norms of beauty, dignity, intelligibility, pertinence to the reality of cult or sacrament, relationship of persons in celebration – ordained ministers who hold the pastoral office, then special lay ministers, and the whole assembly etc.

## CONCLUSION

It needs to be recalled that liturgy celebrates the mystery of salvation which is climaxed in the resurrection of Jesus. What ever that facilitates the effective re-enactment of this mystery should be aggressively pursued for the personal appropriation of the tremendous influence of this great mystery in the life of the church.

Liturgy celebrates in the final analysis, the glorious resurrection power of Jesus with all its overwhelming, far reaching implications and effects. The liturgical celebration of the Resurrection of Jesus proclaims that out of every death, God wills a resurrection. Liturgy proclaims in ritual form that death is swallowed up in victory; that life is changed not ended; that mortality is sucked up in immortality; that corruptibility is subsumed in incorruptibility; that perishability is supplanted by imperishability.

Liturgy reassures the church of this truth and reality. It commemorates this tremendous mystery in the life of the church. It restores this guarantee in the members. It revives their faith and hope in this promise; and re-activates their thoughts accordingly. It re-orientates their world-view in accordance with this saving mystery. It re-directs the church's mentality through worshipping form with regard to her mission in the world. It remodels the life of the church along this paschal mystery of Christ leading to an authentic christian living. It further challenges the church not just to appreciate and admire the glories of the resurrection power of Jesus but also to imitate Him in their lives. Liturgy invites the church unto *anamnesis-mimesis-martes* – a real re-enactment and authentic imitation through witnessing of life.

Liturgy recalls ritually the victory that Jesus has not just won a battle but the whole war; that Jesus is victorious after all said and done as the church carefully experiences in the yearly remembrance of the Holy Week. It professes in praying form, the supreme victory of Christ over sin, death, principalities, forces, powers, thrones, domination, sickness, pains, suffering and satanic influences.

It teaches within the context of celebration that pain and suffering have not only been redeemed, but have acquired salvific signification and thus make them reasonably and purposefully tolerable. Liturgy affirms ritually that out of every death, God destines a new vitality. It confirms in a ritual manner a return to new life by declaring the joyful hope and expectation that revitalise any dead society. Liturgy ritualises the happy result of a great beam of light at the end of a dark tunnel.

The liturgy whose chief act is the eucharistic celebration declares that just as in the eucharistic liturgy particularly at consecration, bread and wine are transformed into the sacred body and blood of Christ, so also at the eucharistic celebration all other human conditions and realities including the worshipping assembly are transformable into better forms. There is no aspect of the human condition that is beyond the scope of the transformative power of the liturgy. In the liturgy the church celebrates the life of Christ. It celebrates the mystery of the church. Liturgy means theology in celebration.

# CHAPTER TWO

# READY TO BUILD A HOUSE OF WORSHIP

## Introduction

It is our good intention here to provide principles and practical pieces of advice to those ready or about to erect a place of worship namely, a church building. Our intention has a further scope of including those wishing to update an already existing church building in the light of the present exigences of satisfying the liturgical requirements, modern age and practical functional utility. It is customary to tell an architect who asks for advice as he begins to plan, design and interpret the plan for a church building what to do. The planning of a liturgical building depends largely on the description of the Altar, the Ambo and the Baptistery and on their unified interrelationship as prescribed by logic and theology.

It has to be borne in mind that erecting a church building has very deep theological implications. Every thing about the building communicates clearly some divine realities which uplift the mind, body and soul to God. Technically, a church building contributes essentially in giving time and space a certain profound theological signification. For instance, space and time, which are the co-ordinates that define human existence in the world, emerge from their formless chaos and produce the formed or ordered world in which humanity lives. Space and time become *here* and *now* and thus acquire a meaning for humanity.

In worship one neither sacralises them as obtainable from pagan point of view nor sanctifies them in the Hebrew manner. In christian liturgy however, they are given new form. Hence for christians, it is by becoming elements of a liturgical celebration that space and time become the *here* and *now* of the paschal mystery, of the historical events of salvation, even while not being cut off in any way from ordinary time and places.

From liturgical point of view then, the specific character of the church as cultic edifice has, neither more nor less, the same relationship to space that the specific character of the christian feast has to amorphous time. Our preoccupation in erecting a befitting church building is one of architecture. It involves shaping space in an orderly and beautiful way by turning it into a place through the liturgical meaning imposed on it. It is envisaged that every church building will lead to greater inculturation. In effect, that there should be churches in every culture by which the churches show forth their identity in form of the cultural values and the genius of their people. Furthermore, the churches must exhibit finer poetic quality. In point of fact, that there be churches representing every kind of aesthetic creativity, with the assistance of which the Holy Spirit will express and effect the marriage of the church and the Word of God in human time and space.

## Nature of a Christian Church Building as a Liturgical Edifice

There exist some basic principles involved in considering a christian church building. A church building is essentially a consecrated building and even without the Eucharist, remains a place where God is specially present and in which the people of God gather to hold their assemblies. The people of God gather here for some specific reasons:

i.      to celebrate and re-enact the sacrificial offering of Christ for human salvation
ii.     to pray
iii.    to receive the fruits of Christ's redemptive sacrifice in the holy sacraments
iv.     to hear the Word of God
v.      to pay their devotions to Christ, present in the eucharistic bread
vi.     to take part in extra-liturgical devotions.

A christian church, however is not merely a place where people gather for liturgical and extra-liturgical functions. It is also a place where the individual christian can make his or her own private devotions. It follows therefore, that on account of the special nature and specific purpose of a church, it ought to deserve certain honour and dignity which it shares with no other building. For instance:

i. A church is in a special way the tabernacle of God among men (Rev. 21:3). It is the place where God guarantees that He may be found by His faithful; it is our Father's House (Lk. 15:17), it is God's royal palace (*basilica*), (*Obi ama Chukwu*). A house of prayer, the house of the Lord as expressed in the fourth century.

ii. It remains a place where the people of God, the Body of Christ, is moulded and developed and so it is a living symbol of this Body. It includes a community of Christ's faithful (cf. Matt.16:18; Col.1:18, 24). A church is in this sense referred to as a domestic church (cf. Acts 2:46).

iii. It continues to be a place in which God's ultimate union with his people is anticipated, and for this reason, therefore, the church building has been rightly described as the heavenly Jerusalem, coming down from heaven to earth (Rev. 21:2).

iv. It stands for a place where the Invisible encounters the visible; and where the Unapproachable is made approachable; where the Infinite meets the finite; where the incorruptibility relates with corruptibility; where the imperishability ennobles the perishability for the divinisation of humanity.

A church is first and foremost a building designed for the offering of the eucharistic sacrifice. This ceremony, however, according to the Western Roman concept of the liturgy, is an action, primarily the action of Christ Himself and of His representative, the celebrating priest, but also an action performed by the whole congregation.

The principal parts taken by the congregation in this sacred action are the responses which precede the preface and the *Amen* at the end of the eucharistic prayer (Canon); the offertory procession and the procession to receive communion. In order that all these actions may be suitably performed, one ideally would want a building fulfilling all these requirements of the Roman liturgy (the interior with the Altar at its focal point, priest and people situated directly opposite one another, making practicable the orderly conduct of procession up and down) without at the same time creating too great a distance between the sanctuary and the far end of the nave. In other words, churches and places of worship should be suited to celebrating the liturgy and to ensuring the active participation of the faithful. It should have all the requisites for worship which must be truly worthy and beautiful, with signs and symbols of heavenly realities.[32]

## Considerations in the Construction of a Church Building

The beauty, the honour and the dignity that should distinguish a befitting place of worship ought to be so evident that at the end of constructing one, both the architect, the people of God and all the major stake holders could well join the psalmist in Ps. 83:1 to sing: *How lovely is your dwelling place, O Lord of hosts.* And again in Ps. 12:1 which says, *...and I rejoiced when I heard them say, Let us go to the house of the Lord.* The worshipping community needs to be proud of their Church building, not as a museum piece but as a central and significant edifice in the midst of other structures in the vicinity. It gives bearing to the other edifices around.

The presence of a church building within any geographical environment becomes a clear dramatisation of the Incarnation: *...and the Word took flesh and dwelt among his people* (Jn. 1:14). Thus within the monotony of a mundane continuum, Divinity makes an indebted and indelible interruption. An interruption that gives Christocentric salvific meaning to space, time and people therein.

It follows however, that by reason of multi-functionality which a church edifice fulfils, its construction opens up a variety of problems. The planning of a church building depends largely on the description and location of the ambo -- for the liturgy of the Word; the Altar for the liturgy of the Eucharist; the celebrant's seat; the baptistery; space for concelebration; accommodation for a projected number of people at a given range and on their unified inter-relationship with the tabernacle; the choir; the press crew; confessional; the blessed Sacrament Chapel; the sacristy; and other conveniences.

Hence, proper planning of a church and its surroundings that meets contemporary needs requires attention not only to the elements belonging directly to liturgical services but also to those facilities for the comfort of the faithful that are usual in places where people are assembled.[33]

# A Gathering Place Near the Church

It needs to be pointed out immediately, that modern church buildings ought to take into consideration the fast and widespread tele-communicational advancements that besiege the modern people. Given the above facilities, it ought to have an elbow reception room at the very entrance where the assembly could gather for a while to shade off the worldliness they carried with them to the church.

The people need such provision where they could easily terminate their conversations and switch off their mobile phones. Otherwise such new tele-communicational devices could constitute a nuisance not only to the owner but also to the entire worshipping community. Such reception room should be furnished with security facilities where people could safely keep their magazines, newspapers etc. until after the celebration.

This may invariably require a forecourt or a proper *atrium* according to the most ancient tradition, thus preparing themselves to enter the silence of the holy place where God is present. It may be a courtyard, a cloister or part of the garden or churchyard or even a suitable hall or a nearby church or chapel. Here the people gather for the processions on February 2nd and Passion (Palm) Sunday. A suitable area near the church is essential if the Easter Vigil is to begin properly. It may also be useful for marriages and funerals and for the *Corpus Christi* procession.[34]

# Designing the Exterior of the Church

It would be incorrect to make the exterior of a church, in proportion, outline, structure and decoration, so like contemporary secular buildings in the immediate vicinity that it appears to be just another secular building. It would be just as wrong as to put up advertising slogans on the wall of the church to attract the attention of passers-by in the street.

Concerted effort should be directed towards pointing out the wholly other, supernatural and divine aspect of what goes on in the interior of the church in a way which is both dignified and expressive and to structure the church in such a manner that it tones in suitably with its immediate environment.

27

## Shape of the Church Building

A factory-like or one trunk edifice could hardly suffice for a church building. Oval structured liturgical edifices would be ideal, such that all could see eye ball to eye ball with the celebrant on the Altar at any corner of the church. A situation where the celebrant at the Altar can hardly see the eye ball of any one at one end of the church is already a small index of a big whole. Rectangular shaped church buildings, or square shaped structures or broad rectangular shaped buildings are rather outmoded.

It should be built to emphasise the family spirit of liturgical celebrations and the importance of the common priesthood of the worshipping community. New churches should therefore be built with a modified centripetal plan – semi-circle in form. The shape ought in a most excellent manner enhance maximum visibility, audibility, unity and simplicity.

## Other Important Facilities

Another important facility is a befitting water closet beside the sacristy. Its importance cannot be over emphasised. A similar facility is to make provision for the noisy or crying infants who disturb now and again during worship. Adequate arrangement should be put in place for such children and their mothers. In this way those who attend to infants and crying babies could still participate by seeing what happens on the Altar and the babies are able to watch and listen to the singing while playing their natural role as infants. In some developed countries of the world, a separate room is designed besides the people's area of the church which is covered with special noise proof glasses. The texture of such glasses are manufactured in a manner that the noise from inside is silent while the noise from outside remains audible.

## Sections of a Church Building

The kind of building needed for the celebration of the Eucharist for instance, is different from that required for the administration of the sacraments of baptism and penance. In effect, one would need one kind of building for administering the sacraments, another for preaching sermons, one for the veneration of the sacrament and yet another for conducting popular devotions and still another for people's private devotions. It is the task of the assembly and her architects to find a solution to the problem of how this variety of usage to which a church is put, can be fulfilled in the most fitting manner possible.

The offering of eucharistic sacrifice, the administration of sacraments, the preaching of the Word, and the veneration of the blessed Lord in the sacraments are not performed in exactly the same way in every christian church in the world. Over the centuries, a variety of methods of performing these tasks, called liturgies or rites, has been evolved. The most important of these liturgies are the Roman and the Byzantine, the former proper to the sees of the West, and the latter to the churches of the East.

Although in essentials, these two rites are wholly in agreement, Roman and Byzantine churches are characterised by certain differences in their outward forms. Hence a church in which the Roman liturgy is to be celebrated cannot be identified with one which has to serve the purposes of the Byzantine liturgy.

## Purpose in Designing a Church

A church is meant for the people of God of the present day. Hence it ought to be designed in such a way that people today may feel that it speaks to their own particular condition. In it the deepest needs of contemporary man and woman should find their fulfilment. Here, their desire to live in community, their demand to know what is true, what is genuine, their desire to escape from what is merely peripheral and to occupy themselves with issues of fundamental importance, their passion for clarity, enlightenment, and lucidity, and their longing for peace and quiet, warmth and shelter is adequately provided.

## Church and Related Structures

However personal this may sound or appear, it would be incorrect to build ones church and school, local hospital and office for social services, parish

29

hall and parish library, presbytery and sacristan's house all in different places unless for want of land or for some other good reasons for doing so. Ideally, one ought to strive after to join all these institutions together in one place in a single harmonious unit, so that people could see clearly the close connection between the church and its clergy, the Eucharist and the administration of charity, and between the sacraments and education.

Schools in this contexts are church owned schools where the church has full control of the curriculum, funding and running the schools. This will enable the church to instil discipline in the schools and maintain the decorum that should exist for a harmonious co existence with the other buildings and offices. Recreation grounds for games should not be a part of the harmonious unit of related structures because of the noise and recreation that go with games.

## Siting A Church Building

It would not be a good idea to situate a church (without good reason) right on the edge of a noisy main thoroughfare, however necessary it may be to direct the attention of the modern people, such as they are in the eyes of this world, very firmly towards the eternal God.

It would be a mistake to abandon without good reason the venerable tradition of building a church to face East.[35] The faithful should be helped to understand and to become conscious of the profound and beautiful symbolism of turning towards the East for prayer, thereby bringing to life once more the direction in which churches today are orientated.

## Interior Design of a Church Building

It would be a mistake not to plan the interior of a church with a view to making it suitable for the offering of the Eucharistic sacrifice, but rather with a view to making it fit for the veneration of the eucharistic presence of Christ. This would be wrong, because in the scale of purposes for which a church is used, the veneration of Christ in the sacrament does not assume the first place.

Ideally, this conflict can only be solved in a satisfactory manner if, there is a place for the offering of the eucharistic sacrifice separate from that where the sacrament is venerated, and also, if possible, separate places should be provided for the sacraments of baptism penance and counselling. If this is done, each section can be architecturally designed to suit its own particular purposes.

It would be incorrect to construct the interior of a church in such a way that the congregation loses its sense of being a unity, a family gathered together for worship. It would, on the other hand, be just as incorrect if the interior were constructed so that there was not a single corner left for people to pray in private.

The best solution to this situation would probably be a church in which on the one hand there is always available an adequate space to contain large congregations on Sundays and feast days and also the smaller week-day congregations particularly for small christian communities, which would serve to emphasise the unity of the assembled congregation. On the other hand it would still have just the kind of corner for devotion that the individual would want for making his or her own private devotional exercises.

It would be a mistake if one were to structure and decorate the church in imitation of the comfort of the houses of the well-to-do or the bareness of the houses of the poor. The interior of an ideal church ought to convey the impression of being neither middle-class nor working-class. It should do something to convey the majesty of God, which is far removed from all secular or mundane standards, and thus lift all who enter out of their private lives while at the same time allowing them to sense the human kindness of God (cf. Titus 3:4).

## Designing the Sanctuary

The sanctuary is the place where the Altar stands, the Word of God is proclaimed, and the priest, the deacon and other ministers exercise their offices.[36] Being the prominent sacred area where most of the ceremonial actions of the liturgy are carried out, it should be spacious, clearly defined and delineated. [37]

Its position, size and elevation has a place in the visibility and audibility requirements for a good functional liturgy. There is no fixed measurement for it. The size of the sanctuary depends comparatively on the size and shape of the church edifice. But generally the length stretching into the church is about 34 feet to 44 feet. The width is greatly conditioned by the shape or form of the wings of the church.[38]

It would be considered incorrect to fill the back wall of the sanctuary with windows so that these cause ones eyes to be distracted from the altar itself. Probably, light coloured windows could be prudently fixed provided that they do not constitute themselves a source of distraction to the worshipping community. It would be just as much a mistake to fill up the back wall with sacred pictures which have no connection with the eucharistic sacrifice, and which are not suitable for the whole of the liturgical year.

Ideally, the architecture and decoration of the sanctuary should be chosen in such a way that ones attention is not drawn to these in themselves but rather to the Altar and to the sacred action which is being performed there. For the danger in putting up pictures and images in the sanctuary is that they distract from the world of imagery created by the solemn eucharistic prayer (namely the text of the Mass, between the *Sursum corda* and the concluding doxology). In any case, people ought not in these matters to have recourse to historical precedent, but should rather choose themes of lasting significance.

The size of the sanctuary should be proportionate to the size of the rest of the building, and the pavement between the altar steps and the altar rails should be wide and deep enough to provide enough room for solemn Mass with a deacon or concelebrants to be celebrated quite smoothly.

It would be incorrect to equip a parish church of average proportions with a sanctuary big enough to take as many clergy as one would find in the chancel of a cathedral. It would be just as wrong to build a sanctuary so short that the altar steps came right up to the altar rails.

The sanctuary is a permanently fixed area, the sacred space reserved for action at the Altar. It is therefore, contrary to sound religious psychology to relocate the sanctuary area from time to time in the course of the year or to place chairs for the faithful in it.[39] Within the sanctuary the following objects are located.

## Altar Area

The Altar area within the sanctuary is very vital in a church building. Ideally it has a minimum dimension of 12 feet x 16 feet. On this platform, the altar table rests. It must allow enough space to walk round the altar.

## Nature of an Altar

The Altar according to its original meaning, is the place where earth is raised up to heaven. In a christian context, the altar is considered to be the table where the people of God offer sacrifice and hold their meal, and at the same time the place where God appears among his people in His Eucharistic Presence. Since however, through consecration, the God-Man becomes present on the Altar, the Altar, even when it has no tabernacle, is also the Throne of Christ. Thus, the Fathers of the Church concluded that it represented Christ Himself, for the throne indeed represents the Ruler. It is the central place of worship symbolic of Christ's presence. It is the table of the Lord (1Cor. 10:21). It ought to be noble, most beautifully designed but simply constructed table of the eucharistic assembly. On it are placed the bread and wine, sacred vessels and book during liturgical celebration.

The main Altar of a church should be a fixed Altar, since it represents Christ Jesus, the Living Stone.[40] However, in other places set aside for sacred celebrations, a moveable altar is permitted. A fixed altar is attached to the floor so that it cannot be moved; a moveable altar is one that can be transferred from place to place.[41] According to biblical symbolism and western tradition, at least the table of a fixed Altar is made of natural stone. Another solid, becoming and skilfully constructed material may be approved by the Episcopal conference.[42] The pedestal or base of the table may be made of any sort of material, as long as it is becoming and solid.[43]

Fixed Altars are solemnly dedicated by a bishop or exceptionally, by a delegated priest. Moveable Altars are blessed by a bishop or authorised priest.[44] The Altar stands at the central axis of the sanctuary.

From all this it follows that it is very wrong to make the Altar look like a shelf set up against the wall or to construct it as if its sole or primary function were to be a support for the tabernacle, crucifix, candles, reliquaries, pictures and small statues.

Furthermore, in the building of new churches, it is especially important that a single altar be erected which signifies to the assembly of the faithful the one Christ and the one Eucharist of the Church. however, in churches already built when an old altar is already so positioned that it makes the participation of the people difficult or it is impossible to move it without detriment to its artistic value, then another fixed altarmay be erected.[45] Here the same procedure for a fixed altar is to be followed.

The practice of placing under the altar to be dedicated relics of saints, even of non martyrs is to be maintained. Care must be taken to have solid evidence of the authenticity of such relics especially an identifiable part of the body of a saint.[46]

## Location of an Altar

In an ideal church the Altar should be set in an isolated position, raised up in proportion to the rest of the building, free standing and arranged in such a way that people could walk round it. It has to be carefully planned and designed. The material of which it is made has to be wisely selected. Its monumentality in comparison with the proportions of the rest of the building, the way in which the perspectives of the interior neatly converge upon it must be taken into serious consideration. Its location within the most brightly lit part of the church should show clearly that the altar is the holiest place in the church. It is the very heart and centre of everything in the church. The altar in fact should be the starting point from which the ideal church should be planned and structured, both as to its interior as to its exterior design.

In larger churches, it would be wrong to situate the altar for no particular reason at the very end of the building as so often happened in early christian times in churches built in the form of a hall (single room churches) or factory like church building. One would be more in accordance both with tradition and with the present-day circumstances if one were to make a separate sanctuary or choir for the altar, rectangular, hemispherical, or polygonal in shape (a two-room church).

It would be a pity if in the building used for worship ones attention were distracted from the altar by side altars, statues, stations of the Cross, confessionals, clumsily placed candle-stands, and pews which all serve to distract the attention of the faithful from the holy things themselves. Consequently, all superfluous additions should be dispensed with, and necessary structures, for instance, side altars and confessionals, should, where possible, be relegated to side chapels or to a crypt. What remains in the main body of the church should be constructed and arranged so as not to interrupt the gentle flow of the interior up to the altar.

## The Furnishings of the Altar

At least one white cloth should be placed on an Altar where Mass is celebrated out of reverence for the celebration of the memorial of the Lord and the banquet that gives us his body and blood. The shape, size and decoration of the altar should be in keeping with the design of the altar.[47]

This cloth should not be confused with a coloured *antependium*. Although not obligatory, an *antependium,* or frontal, enhances the dignity of the altar. A fixed marble altar with liturgical designs serves as an exception in this matter of covering an altar Together with a matching lectern fall and tabernacle veil, it clearly defines the season by changing the whole setting for the celebration in a harmonious but vivid way.[48]

The cross should be located on, next to, immediately behind or suspended above the altar. In the context of the Roman liturgy, cross means a crucifix.[49] A figure of the risen Christ behind an altar cannot be regarded as a substitute for the cross, however there is a wide range of styles of figures to choose from which may be suitable for the liturgical crucifix.[50] Ideally, there should be one cross at a celebration.

## Ceremonial Area

The ceremonial area is the platform immediately before the Altar. It is most useful when ordinations, religious professions, holy week especially Good Friday and similar activities take place. A minimum space of 8 feet (2500 mm) is required for this measuring from the Altar platform to the last landing (step) into the sanctuary.[51]

## Altar Steps

A minimum number of two steps is required between the communion platform and the ceremonial platform. The step (risers) measures 6 inches high (150mm) and 15 inches (375 mm) wide each.[52]

## Communion Space

The space between the last step of the Altar and the communion rail is equally of vital importance. It should be roomy enough to allow for ceremonies on the rail e.g. communion distribution, ash distribution, blessing and imposition of hands on the people etc. A minimum width space of 4 feet (1300mm) is normally suitable for the communion space. An additional 12 inches (300mm) is required for fixing the communion railing as well as providing enough kneeling space for communicants. The riser is about 6 inches high (150mm). The railing is necessary to provide support for the weak, the aged and enhance order in the flow of people for communion and other exercises. The kneeling step could be padded to provide minimum kneeling comfort. The materials for the railing could be wooden, concrete or marble, but each must be of high quality and with good finishing.

## Location of the Sacristy

It would be a mistake not to situate the sacristy right next to the sanctuary and to place it, as in early christian times, at one side of the west front of the church. It would, on the other hand, be a good idea if a connecting passage were constructed between the sacristy and the entrance to the church so that on Sundays and feast days the clergy could process solemnly through the congregation up to the altar, the Introit chant of the eucharistic liturgy thereby regaining its full signification.

While not strictly part of the liturgical setting, the sacristy plays an important role in the preparations for worship and in its worthy accomplishment. According to European tradition, the major sacristy is a kind of chapel and may even include a fixed altar. It should be adequately spacious in relation to the size of the church. A distinct vesting room near the door to the church is desirable.[53]

A crucifix or some other sacred image should be the central focus of the major sacristy, as this is customarily venerated by the clergy and the servers before and after liturgical celebrations.

A card should be displayed bearing the names of the Pope and the diocesan bishop and the title of the church, for the information of visiting celebrants. Holy water should be available in a stoup at the door into the church. A bell may be hung on the wall near this door to alert the people when a procession is about to enter the church.[54]

In designing or renovating a sacristy, the following details should be kept in mind:

i.    a spacious table or bench for setting out vestments

ii.    ample cupboards and drawers

iii.    a secure safe for sacred vessels and the tabernacle key

iv.    a sink with flowing water (hot and cold as the case may be) and towels

v.    a second small sink leading directly into the earth (sacrarium or piscina)

vi.    a place for storing bread and wine

vii.    a bookcase for the liturgical books

viii.    safer custody for sacramental registers,

ix.    a fixed place for the current Ordo or calendar

x.    a clock

xi.    a bracket for the processional cross

xii.    a place for reserving the Eucharist during the Easter ceremonies

xiii.    a repository or aumbry for the Holy Oils, if they are not kept in the baptistery.[55]

xiv.    Inside the *sacristy* there should be:

xv.    a large sink with a flowing water (hot and cold)

xvi.    holy water container

xvii. an ironing board and iron

xviii. storage for a vacuum cleaner

xix. a polisher

xx. cleaning materials

xxi. storage space for candlesticks, candelabra, the Easter candle stand

xxii. crib figures

xxiii. church supplies such as candles, votive candles, oil or wax lamp re-fills incense, charcoal, last year's palms.

xxiv. A refrigerator may be useful.

xxv. A fireproof area where thuribles are kept and prepared should be in or near the sacristy. However, the servers and a robbed choir should have their own separate vesting room.[56]

## Cleanliness and Order

Regarding cleanliness and order in the sacristy, these should be religiously maintained as are essential in the care of the church itself. Special care should be taken of decorative objects, vessels and vestments handed on from the past, except for objects of no great value which are beyond repair or refurbishing.[57]

## Silence in the Sacristy

Silence before and after a liturgical celebration should be required of all who assist in the sacristy.[58] The mystery that is about to be celebrated requires naturally the maintenance of prayerful silence. The same degree of silence would be required also after the celebration.

## Location of the Baptismal Font

At holy baptism members are born again as children of God and at the same time made members of the Church, the body of Christ. It is lamentable that in parish churches today, this fundamental meaning of the sacrament of rebirth is scarcely expressed at all, and as a result, the font is one of the most neglected features of the church.

In an ideal church, a place specially partitioned off ought to be given to the font, which itself should be monumental in form and situated near the entrance to the church. Other possible places of situating it include in the middle of the congregation and thirdly near the altar, in clear view of the people and large enough to accommodate many people.[59] There is a venerable tradition which directs that this space should be either round or polygonal in shape. If one reflects a moment on the baptismal rite itself, then one shall come to the conclusions concerning the structure of the baptistery. For the very heart of the baptismal rite is not so much that man is performing an action, but rather that he is the object and recipient of the secret activity of God. For a rite with this kind of content, a long building, which suggests symbolically a building meant for action, is inappropriate and so one requires rather a building with its focal point at the centre, its axis running vertically up and down, thus symbolising a place where the grace of God is received.

Since baptism by immersion is regarded as the fuller and more appropriate symbolic act of administering baptism, it is recommended that new baptismal fonts be reconstructed to allow for the immersion of infants so that water can be poured over the whole body of the infant, and even of adults. The size is a matter of choice and suitability for the purpose it is meant to serve and adequately too. The font is to have a cover to prevent the receptacle from insects and dust. The decoration should be symbolically rich in salvific liturgical history.

## Location of Pews and Gangways

It would be wrong to fill up the nave with pews to such an extent that the front ones come right up to the altar or communion rails, and that the side ones reached nearly to the wall.

In a standard church, provision should be made for sufficiently wide gangways to be kept in the centre, at the sides, in front of the altar rails, and at the entrance, so that if several hundreds wish to come to the Lord's Table, there will be no un-edifying crush. A spacious nave facilitates processions ordered for certain liturgical occasions (namely the Introit procession on Sundays and feast days and the processions on Candle Mass and Palm Sunday, etc) may be performed without people being cramped for space.

The space between the pews should be large enough to allow convenient kneeling. Entry into the seats from two ends is advisable. The sitting arrangements must ensure at least adequate spaces for movement. The central aisle should measure at least 4 feet; while the side aisles should have a minimum of 3 feet space.

## Location of the Tabernacle

The tabernacle relates to the altar as the basket of fragments to the scene of the multiplication of the loaves and fishes (Jn. 6). It retains the fruits of the sacred action when Mass is over for the communion of the sick and for the private devotion of the faithful. The blessed sacrament should be reserved in a tabernacle in a part of the church which is noble, prominent, worthy, beautifully decorated and suitable for prayer.[60]

As a rule, there should be only one tabernacle, immovable, made of solid and unbreakable material and not transparent, and locked so that the danger of desecration is avoided as much as possible.[61] It is suitable that the tabernacle be blessed, before it is considered for liturgical use, according to the rite described in the Roman ritual.

Considerable discussions continue concerning the location of the tabernacle. However, all the official instructions during and since the Second Vatican Council need to be interpreted in the light of Canon 938 par. 2 of the 1983 Code of Canon Law which states: the tabernacle in which the blessed Eucharist is reserved should be sited in a distinguished place in a church or oratory, a place which is conspicuous, suitably adorned and conducive to prayer.[62]

The location of the tabernacle should never be confused with the location of the Altar. The former remains a befitting place of reservation of the blessed Eucharist, while the later is the locus for consecrating the blessed Eucharist. As said above, the Altar is the centre of any church, a place of divine manifestation, where the miracle of consecration of bread and wine takes place to become the body and blood of Christ. It is a privileged locus of divine encounter with his people. It is the locus where God feeds his people with his body and blood. The internal arrangement of the structures within a church must bear this in mind. It must ensure that the prominent place of each of this is not blurred by the other.

It seems best however, in some way to retain a visible link between the altar and tabernacle, between celebration and adoration, between action and reservation. This could well be achieved by:

i.    relocating the tabernacle behind the altar.

ii.    placing a new altar in an eucharistic chapel which had none before and thus creating a space for intimate celebrations.

iii.    reserving the Eucharist on a noble and conspicuous side altar.

The first provision looks unacceptable in the light of the spirit of the reformed liturgy of the Second Vatican Council which favours the last two provisions.

It would be incorrect to locate the tabernacle within the sanctuary whereby the tendency of clash of symbols will be evident. Just as it is wrong to locate the tabernacle in the sanctuary whereby concelebrants would be compelled to back it during the celebration of the liturgy. It would be equally wrong to locate the tabernacle where there is regular traffic. It is argued that the tabernacle would constitute a distraction during liturgical celebrations, therefore, the area for celebration must be separate from the area for reservation. Furthermore, it has also been argued hat the separate eucharistic chapel promotes devotion to the Blessed Sacrament.

Ideally, Eucharistic chapel would be most preferable. This requires the creation of a separate chapel, or area apart from the sanctuary as the only correct place for the tabernacle.

The place of reservation is to be suitably adorned, for aesthetics also makes this place conducive to prayer. Suitable adornment may include the primary sign of reservation, a noble veil or canopy, suggesting the mystery of God tabernacling among his people, the tent of the Lord. Placing a beautiful lamp near the tabernacle, with appropriate artificial lightening (preferably natural light) also enhances the setting for eucharistic reservation. The adornment should express the glory of the Lord, without detracting from the tabernacle itself. Where a eucharistic chapel is justified, let it be not only splendid but spacious, hence conducive to the prayer of more than a few people.[63]

Each pastor may wish to look at the location of the tabernacle in his church and ask himself whether this is really a distinguishing place, conspicuous, suitably adorned and conducive to prayer. He may also put this question to his people who use the church.[64]

In resolving any matter which affects the spiritual life of many people, one should be guided by the Second Vatican Council. One should listen with great sensitivity to the *sensus fidei* of the faithful. A pastoral understanding of the faith of the people of God reveals the need to rethink this question seriously. Devotion to the blessed Lord in the Eucharist is embedded in the religious psyche of the people. It is not an optional-extra for devout souls. This devotion remains essential to the continuity of the living tradition not only of the Rite but of the Faith itself. The perception was captured in the words of Pope Paul VI, when he described the tabernacle as the living heart of each of our churches.[65]

In order to promote prayer and reverence, let the Eucharist be restored to the truly pre-eminent position in every church. Where this has happened, the response of the faithful has been a resurgence of devotion to the eucharistic Lord. Through the incarnation, human way of affirming priorities through signs and symbols, let Jesus be seen to be who he is – the centre of the faith and love, the summit and source (*culmen et fons*) of the life of the Church.[66]

The importance of discussion cannot be over-stressed. It helps a great deal in informing ones decision especially where the final decision regarding the location of the tabernacle lies on the judgement of the local ordinary. The tabernacle should be placed, according to the judgement of the diocesan bishop: either in the sanctuary, apart from the altar of celebration, in the most suitable form and place, not excluding on an old altar which is no longer used for celebration. or even in another chapel suitable for adoration and private prayer of the faithful, and which is integrally connected with the church and is conspicuous to the faithful.[67]

If placed in the sanctuary, it must stand on a level higher than the altar table. Two steps of risers 6 inches x 15 inches (150mm x 375 mm) are required to the final landing. The landing dimension shall be a minimum of

3 feet 6 inches (1050 mm) to allow enough space for genuflection and other services on the platform. The tabernacle altar table should have a minimum of 3 feet (900 mm) to accommodate the tabernacle and allow sufficient space on the table for reservation and bringing out the sacred species.

A lamp should burn continuously near the tabernacle to signify the real presence of Christ, as a sign of reverence and honour to Christ, and as a symbol of the rich blessings that emanate from there. The light should be of natural oil or wax (candle) to symbolise truly the supernatural and living effects being evoked.[68]

## The Ambo/Lectern

The dignity of the word of God requires the church to have a place that is suitable for proclamation of the word and is a natural focal point for the faithful during the liturgy of the word.

There is to be one preferably permanent ambo [69] not simply a movable stand for the proclamation of the word of God from or near the sanctuary. By tradition and favoured practice, it may be in a fixed position to the left of the altar (facing the altar) on what was called the Gospel side. However, the distinctive plan of a church or the choir liturgy of a religious community or seminary may require a different place for the ambo. It should be designed to harmonise with, but never to overshadow, the altar. The ambo may be covered with a dignified *antependium* or fall of the colour of the day or season, preferably matching the *antependium* on the altar.

The ambo must be placed so that the ordained ministers and readers may be easily seen and heard by the faithful. The readings, responsorial psalm and the Easter Proclamation (*Exultet*) are proclaimed ideally only from the ambo; it may be used also for the homily and general intercessions (prayer of the faithful). The dignity of the ambo requires that only a minister of the word should approach it.[70] Before use, every ambo requires a blessing using the appropriate liturgical rite for it.

If possible, the surface where the book rests should be adjustable, to meet the needs of readers, including children. In most churches a reliable microphone and good lightening will be required. A shelf or cupboard may be built into the ambo for books. The area around it must allow room for the candle bearers and thurifer at the reading of the Gospel and also for the Easter candle, which is set up near the ambo during the Easter season. The homilist should be able to see a clock from the ambo.[71] A cantor, choir director, announcer or commentator should not use the ambo reserved for the proclamation of the word of God.[72] It would be an abuse to use the lectern for fund raising or other secular projects.

## The Chair for the Priest Celebrant and Other Chairs

The chief celebrant's chair ought to stand as a symbol of his function of presiding over the assembly and of directing prayer. Thus the best place for the chair is at the head of the sanctuary and turned toward the people, unless the design of the building or other circumstances are an obstacle, for example, if too great a distance would interfere with communication between the priest and the gathered assembly, or if the tabernacle is positioned medially behind the altar. However, anything resembling a throne is to be avoided.[73] It is appropriate that the chair be blessed before it is designated for liturgical use. This should be done according the rite described in the Roman ritual.

In the same way, chairs may be placed in the sanctuary for priest concelebrants and all other priests who are present for the celebration in clerical dress (Soutane) but are not concelebrating. The seats for the deacon should be placed near that of the celebrant. However, the seats for the other ministers should be arranged so that they are clearly distinguished from the seats for clergy and, so that the ministers are easily able to fulfil the office assigned to them.[74] In making the chair, the comfort of the celebrant should not be forgotten.

## The Bishop's Chair

In a Cathedral, the cathedra is a throne reserved for bishops. The cathedra should be raised on steps so that the bishop is clearly visible when he presides in his own church. A separate chair must be provided for a priest who is the celebrant at the main altar of a cathedral.

Seats may be placed on either side of the chair or the cathedra for deacons and perhaps for an instituted acolyte and the master of ceremonies at solemn functions. The seats for concelebrants must be assured. The servers should never occupy these places. If possible, servers should not sit facing the people, as if they were presiding. Chairs, stools or benches should be provided for them in the sanctuary itself, [75] preferably near the credence table and along the sides. However, the sanctuary should never be cluttered up with chairs, benches or prie-deux (praying or kneeling desks).[76]

Very importantly, a server holds the book when the celebrant reads any text at the chair. A simple lectern placed in front of the chair may be tolerated only during a Mass celebrated without servers.[77] Some one else will be assigned with the role of holding microphones.

## Nave/Places For the Faithful

Whatever may be the design of a church, the area for the people is designated as the nave.[78] The places for the faithful should be arranged with care so that they are able to take their rightful part in the celebration visually and mentally. As a rule, there should be benches or chair for their use. But the custom of reserving seats for private persons must be abolished.[79]

Especially in newly built churches, however, benches or chairs should be set up in such a way that the people can easily take the postures required during various parts of the celebration and have unimpeded access to receive communion. There should be enough room for worshippers to stand and kneel conveniently. Therefore, whatever form the seats take, they should be spaced carefully and equipped with some form of comfortable kneeler.[80] The faithful must be enabled not only to see the priest, the deacon and the readers but also, with the aid of modern sound equipment, to hear them without difficulty.[81]

## The Choir and Musical Instruments in the Nave

In relation to the design of each church, the *schola cantorum* should be so placed that its character as a part of the assembly of the faithful that has a special function stands out clearly. The location should also assist the exercise of the duties of the *schola cantorum* and allow each member of the choir to have complete participation, that is, sacramental participation in the Mass.[82]

The organ and other lawfully approved musical instruments are to be located in a suitable place where they can sustain the singing of the choir and congregation and be heard by all with ease when they are played alone. It is appropriate that the organ be blessed before its designation for liturgical use. This should be done according to the rite described in the Roman Ritual.[83] Expert advice should be sought when locating the choir in order to promote its indispensable role in Catholic worship. The Second Vatican Council explicitly endorsed the place of the organ in the Roman Rite.[84]

In an ideal church, which is organised and structured in accordance with the best liturgical interests, the choir should be given a place in the nave, right next to the sanctuary. In order not to abandon the galleries at the back altogether, they should be used for certain category of the assembly. In a typical overcrowded country churches, they could be reserved for youths or children.

Secondly, they could be used for the organ, the liturgical function of which does not consist in filling in pauses in the sacred action with solo music, but rather in supporting the singing of the choir and congregation, and, on occasions, in lending weight to the festal mood of the people at the beginning and end of the liturgical function.

The gallery at the back would also be the normal place for the four-part polyphonic choir and orchestra, though the last of these is quite clearly alien to strictly liturgical services.

## Chapel or Chapels in the Nave

In an ideal church provision should be made for a chapel or chapels, but not for a multiplicity of altars. Shrines for the devotion of the faithful to Our Lady and the saints have their place, without detracting from the liturgy. Therefore, sacred images set up for the devotion of the faithful should not be placed permanently in the sanctuary. Restraint should be exercised in the number and arrangement of sacred images, and two images of the same saint should not be included in the same building. This need not necessarily preclude images of Our Lady under different titles or other representations of a saint included in a group of figures.[85]

## Confessional in the Nave

Normally near the nave, confessionals are provided for the celebration of the Sacrament of Penance (according to the first and second rites of reconciliation).

In modern practice, these are pleasant and reasonably spacious soundproof rooms, equipped with a chair, a kneeler and with a crate, screen or grille, between the priest and penitent, as the Code requires.[86] Where the bishops allow it, the room should be designed so that the penitent may also choose the option of *face to face* confession.[87] The confessional should be located at the back of the Church or any other suitable place where a possible connection could be made to the Altar.

## Stations of the Cross

The Stations of the Cross are usually placed in the nave, or in a chapel or area where the faithful may easily make the devotion. The practice of grouping all the Stations closely together at one point is unfortunate because it eliminates the significant movement from place to place which is part of this devotion.

Each Station should be identifiable with very clear symbol. Stations are to be blessed by a bishop or priest, but a new set of Stations erected in a church about to be dedicated is blessed by the act of dedication – as are the font, cross, images and statues, organ, bells, etc. in that place.[88] The Stations should not be confused with the twelve or four crosses set onto or into the walls of a dedicated church.[89]

## Place For The Communications Media – The Press

One feature which is very often forgotten in church building is a fixed or permanent place for the agents of the media. In planning a church edifice this too should be included in the structural plan. The media have an important role to play in the society and even more in the church. The absence of this fixed place for them compel them to jump from one place to the other in an attempt to cover the ceremony as much as possible. To run after them in the church during a liturgical celebration simply confirms that one has failed to plan well. Even in the churches that have been completed already, there is still room to carve out a permanent place for the press crew.[90]

## Bell Tower

Right through the ages the bell has tolled to rally people to church, to give message of death of a member, to recall the angelic message of the coming of the Redeemer, to create a consciousness of time of a celebration and even to rally the faithful in times of danger and of celebration. It reminds the people also to pray the *Angelus* at morning, noon and dusk.

Against this backdrop every church ought to have a bell tower well erected. In line with modern thought and in the steps of the Second Vatican Council, the bell tower is constructed a little distance away from the actual church edifice with a covered corridor or walkway connecting the two.[91] According to the longstanding custom of the Latin Church, new bells are solemnly blessed before they are hung in a belfry or campanile.[92] Those who ring the bells should be trained properly.

## Gallery

Higher level galleries may be recommended for construction inside churches, particularly where there are limitations of sitting spaces as well mentioned above. The galleries may be located at the sides or rear end of the church. In whichever area the galleries are located, the slabs must maintain adequate gentle slope towards the altar in order to ensure clear visibility of the altar from any corner of the gallery.[93]

## Roof

High-pitched roof is recommended for all churches. A minimum slope of 30 feet (9000 mm) is most advisable, in order to guard against leakage and minimise regular roof maintenance.[94]

## Concrete Roof Slab

Concrete roof gutters, parapets and other forms of roof slabs should be played down. Minor or excessive leakage involved in those elements in the churches where they are introduced make for ugly scenes.[95]

## Pillars

Pillars are required to support the entire church structure. The number of external and internal pillars depends on the complexity of the church design and architecture. For those involved in the design of modern churches care must be exercised to ensure that the faithful enjoy full participation in the liturgical celebrations with their eyes and minds. The pillars must be few inside the church, and possibly completely avoided at the sanctuary.[96]

Qualified professionals must be involved in achieving the structural demand of modern church architecture. The pillars inside the church should have minimum sizes with adequate reinforcements, depending on the relevant spans between effective pillars. Use of steel rafters for roof need to be encouraged, in order to give its advantages against the span limitations of timber and wood.[97]

## Doors

Churches must have enough doors, ensure easy access into and out of the church. The doors must ensure quick exit of the faithful out of the church without undue queues. The number of doors depends entirely on the size of the church. Doors are expected to retain a good overall width and height of minimum 3000m. Doors must be imbued with liturgical art, both on the inside and outside faces in order to inspire devotion in the faithful.[98]

In accord with the common tradition of the East and the West, the major doors of the church should be of noble design, appropriately representing Christ the Way to the Kingdom, the door into the sheepfold of his faithful flock. A ramp and handrails for the infirm and the disabled should be provided to give them access to a door to the church.[99]

A spacious narthex, or porch as said earlier is a useful area at the main door of the church. There may also be direct access from the narthex or the church itself to parish halls or to a social area. While this has obvious pastoral advantages, care should be taken to keep that area distinct from the church and to provide soundproofing if necessary.[100]

## Windows

Windows are very important part of the church. The type and number of windows in a church determine the acceptability of a church design. There must be as many window openings as possible in order to ensure a high degree of ventilation. Generally, low and high level lines of windows are advisable, depending on the overall height of the church. Moderate security fittings with good aesthetics should form part of the construction of windows and doors.[101]

## Tower

The height of towers oughtt be at least 5m (15 feet) above the overall height of the church roof. It is very important that the foundations of towers be carefully designed considering the ultimate load expected from the modern types of bells. Permanent ladder or stair case access must be provided at the last inner level of the tower. Adequate devices must be provided at the last level to take the bells, particularly when the type of bell to be mounted is not known.[102]

## Other Liturgical Areas

Chapels that are used for the celebration of the Eucharist with the people should include an ambo and a presidential chair. Moreover in churches with several altars, one may be set aside for the celebration of the Eucharist without the people, for example, by visiting clergy but not during the principal Mass.

Existing altars which are never or rarely used for the Eucharist should nonetheless be treated with the reverence and respect due to a dedicated altar. They should at least be covered with a cloth or dust-cover, and only liturgical ornaments should be placed on them. In practice, such altars often serve as shrines for popular devotion. However, when a new side altar where the Eucharist is to be celebrated is erected in honour of a saint, the image of that saint is not to be placed directly above the altar.[103]

## Need For Constant Repairs

A stitch in time saves nine applies very well to any church building. It will be most ideal to include the regular maintenance of a church building in the annual budget. Specific amount of money should be devoted towards the constant repair of any part of the building that calls attention for that. This should always be skilfully done so that the repaired part will not disfigure the original aesthetics of the building in any way. Regular periodic painting of the church will help a great deal in keeping the structure always new.

## CONCLUSION

The genuine quest of the holy people of God has to be respected by architects while erecting a church. Build us a church for the liturgy as we celebrate it and as we understand it is always the vocal and or silent demand of the faithful. This has been the central point in the construction of a church. Secondly, to design a satisfactory structure for the liturgy of the people of their own time has been the perennial challenge to church architects at every time in history.People often read ideas into the finished churches just as much as interpreters read ideas into the liturgy when explaining liturgical actions. Care must be taken, therefore of keeping primary purposes and subsequent interpretations well apart.

A finished church building ought to be optimally functional and attractive to the people in terms of drawing them towards it for joyful divine worship. In effect, the faithful need to be as near as possible to the Altar in order that they may watch the sacred actions, and fully understand the words of the liturgy. Liturgy demands that there should be a lively flow of words and actions between the celebrant and the people, and not that the assembly should remain lost in contemplation where they stand as one watching an unfamiliar and incomprehensible movie.

A standard church that meets the time and taste should be such that the entire structure is so fashioned to let in sufficient light in the interior of the church. Nothing should suggest a tendency to divide or separate the congregation at worship. It is intended that nothing should distract the worshipping assembly from the sacred actions at the altar. Hence the simplicity of the walls and ceiling; hence the disappearance of disturbing windows behind the altar; hence the sparing use of sculpture and painting etc.

It should be constantly recalled that the altar remains the focal point of the church and the congregation. The simpler the better as opposed to the attempt to make it look like a monument or too much like a gigantic tomb. At each time a church must provide enough accommodation for the worshipping community. A christian church cannot and must not ignore the fact of salvation. The liturgy of the church stands in the very centre of salvation history.

In any attempt to construct a model church, one should not only work out a plan for the building itself, but also a plan of how the church is to be fitted out from the aesthetic point of view, a plan moreover, which has been well thought out both theologically, (liturgically) and catechetically. Such a plan will consequently ensure that when the church is completed, its decorations will present the faithful not merely with fragments of the spiritual life, but in a certain sense, with the spiritual life as a whole, set out in a logical order with the emphasis in the right place.

Ideally, a church should be just so large that the priest at the altar can be clearly understood and seen without the help of technical equipment even by those sitting at the back rows of the congregation, so that communication, communion of word and sacrament may be given to all in church without disrupting the celebration of Mass itself. This optimum size should not be exceeded without good reason, without prejudice to cathedrals and churches at shrines which need to be somewhat of larger proportions.

Those entrusted with the task of building a church have indeed a heavy responsibility laid upon them. The success of their work depends on whether the faithful love their parish church or do not love it, whether they come to it willingly or unwillingly. One can never be too conscientious, therefore, or too thorough in the planning of a new church.[104] In the final analysis, the people must be able to have some joy and pride in their church as a place of worship. A timely maintenance culture will definitely ensure the longevity of a standard modern church building.

# CHAPTER THREE

# INCULTURATED EUCHARISTIC LITURGY:

# A PROPOSAL

## Introduction

Eucharistic celebration lies at the centre of Sunday as the Day of the Lord. How can one really develop the celebration of Sunday in such a way that the full and true sense of celebration would be remarkably effected within a given local context? It is becoming almost a common feature today especially in some mission lands like Nigeria that what appears to be inculturation features most prominently only during the special offerings at Sunday eucharistic celebration. The simple reason for this assertion is that people open up themselves more at this point in time during the celebration by dancing to the collection boxes to offer their cash offering as often as they are called upon to donate generously. They are prepared to do this, even if it means changing the money into many lower denominations in order to dance as often as the demands are made of them to come and give.

Some are even encouraged to stand up and come to the collection box and offer themselves in case they have nothing to offer (*I nweghi ihe obuna nye ya onwe gi)*. The music is usually more lively, more touching and very exciting. Everyone, including the celebrant, irrespective of the crowd spilling over outside the Church building remains calm. It usually lasts relatively long especially when everyone has to match before the altar amidst dancing and clapping to the rhythm of the loud music. Apart from giving each person a chance to offer something to God, this method prevails over the antiquated secret-bag-collection method which today yields poor financial results. On the other hand, this new method brings in more money.

E. Uzukwu describes this method of offering as a striking adaptation among the *Igbo* people of Nigeria. He describes it further as introducing

*Igbo* patterns of co-operative development or improvement unions into the rite of the presentation of gifts during the eucharistic celebration.[105] The presentation of gifts or offerings in procession, according to the Roman rite, involves bringing the bread and wine to the altar accompanied by the offertory song. Money or gifts for the poor and the Church may also be collected or brought forward during the preparation of gifts.[106] For *Ndigbo*, this has been converted into a procession of song and dance by everybody in the assembly to present his or her gift to the Lord. It has become a fund-raising strategy to ensure a self-reliant church. Offertory hymns are care-fully worked to inspire participation. The procession is accompanied by singing, hand-clapping, and dancing.

The minister often stands before the altar to sprinkle holy water on those presenting their gifts. The most dramatic display of this kind of pres-entation of gifts is on Holy Thursday Cathedraticum/Chrism Mass. Here Parishes, sodalities, religious communities and organisations within the diocese come forward with gifts of all kinds. Bishops who may have reser-vations about charismatic hymns, hand-clapping, dancing and percussion evocative of jazz encourage or allow the free performance of these in order to generate as much revenue as possible.[107] This method of offering is spreading like wild fire across the country and is no longer restricted to *Ndigbo*.

This segment of the eucharistic celebration displays reasonably the sentiments and the genius of the people. It comes closest to the people's heart and makes them active participants in the celebration. The emotion dies down again at the commencement of the eucharistic Prayer. What ap-pears most important here is the people's latent quest to shift from the Ro-man rite of offering to the local way of raising fund for any special project.

In effect, that would be a little index of a big whole, namely a clear manifestation of a genuine yearning to spread the same local approach where possible to the other parts of the celebration. The healthy vibration one experiences during the offertory could be well extended to the various parts of the same celebration so that the celebration becomes fully cultural and at the same time truly Christian.

Would it be possible then to evolve an inculturated eucharistic cele-bration, whereby the lively sentiments exhibited only at the time of the special offertory be extended to all parts of the celebration? One envisages not only the inevitable re-adjustment of the present Order of Mass to be tailored against the people's background but also to be enriched with the authentic cultural values and sentiments of the people. The liturgical principles already abound which lend support to such creativity and innovation.[108] Against this background an honest attempt could be made as a proposal towards an inculturated Order of Mass for a local church like the church in Igbo land.

## Possibility of a New Order of Eucharistic Celebration

One of the laudable achievements of the reformed liturgy of the Second Vatican Council appears visible in the acceptance of its limitations to satisfy all peoples belonging to the Roman rite and thus offers ample opportunities for its improvement or even creating entirely new rites.[109] It took five long years to revise the present order of Mass. In his posthumous book *La riforma liturgica* Annibale Bugnini describes in great detail the various phases of the revision from the first meeting of the study group in April 1964 to the publication of the new *editio typica* on April 3, 1969.[110] What appears to be in question at this juncture would be the possibility of creating an alternative Order of Mass that suits the mentality and the sentiments of the people.

SC. 50 states that the rite of the Mass is to be revised in such a way that the intrinsic nature and purpose of its several parts, as well as the connection between them, may be more clearly manifested, and that devout and active participation by the faithful may be more easily achieved. The text above gives two main reasons why the order of Mass needed revision. The first is in order to restore liturgical celebration to its pristine clarity; the second is in order to foster active participation. In effect, what is needed is ritual clarity and active participation. In the first place what our quest aims at goes beyond revision because the term revision had specific meaning in the minds of the Fathers of the liturgical reforms. For them revision deals with the new traits which the Roman liturgy had acquired when it migrated into Gaul or the Franco-Germanic world in the eighth century.

The second paragraph of the number further reads thus: For this purpose the rites are to be simplified, due care being taken to preserve their substance. Parts which with the passage of time came to be duplicated, or were added with little advantage, are to be omitted. Other parts which suffered loss through accidents of history are to be restored to the vigour they had in the days of the holy Fathers, as may seem useful or necessary.

The thrust of this second paragraph could well be said to be a process of restoration of liturgy to the classical original form. The article lays down three operational principles which clearly echo the recommendations of the preparatory commission. First, the rites are to be simplified without injury to their substance. Second, elements that came to be duplicated or were introduced but with little advantage are now to be discarded. Third, the traditional elements that disappeared from the order of Mass in the course of time should be restored to their former vigour, as may seem useful or necessary. The basic issue is that the Fathers were dealing with restoring an existing rite which found itself somehow mutilated on account of contact with other worlds. The issue of our study incidentally goes beyond revising, restoring an existing rite, but rather to create an alternative which must not be absolutely unconnected with the one existing hitherto.

The basic questionable issue remains to be examined namely, must there be a single order of Mass for everyone irrespective of one's cultural values and the genius of the people? Even for the Fathers of the reformed liturgy one could ask why the reluctance to have more than one order of Mass? At this time of the council, the idea of alternative orders of Mass was surely regarded as a deviation from the long-standing tradition of the Roman rite.[111] The tradition includes the fact that in 1604 Pope Clement VIII justified a uniform celebration of the Eucharist, invoking the principle of church unity. Pope Paul VI himself explained that St. Pius V offered it (the *editio princeps* of the Roman Missal) to the people of Christ as the instrument of liturgical unity.[112]

But according to A. J. Chupungco, times even for the church have changed. After the Council, the experience of local churches in the area of cultural adaptation, especially in the missions, has instilled into consciousness that church unity does not have to be anchored exclusively on the uniform observance of the liturgical rites.[113] Furthermore, even if SC. 50 does

58

not deal directly with cultural adaptation or inculturation, its program of classical restoration has opened new horizons for cultural adaptation. By advocating the restoration of the classical form, it unwittingly recreated an eighth-century situation. In short, it has given to the local churches the occasion , or one might say a perfect excuse, to do with the new order of Mass what the Franco-Germanic Churches did with the order of Mass they received from Rome in the eighth century.[114]

## Preliminaries

1.  The proposals set out here are intended to apply to special celebrations, solemnities and special Sunday Eucharistic celebrations like Fathers day celebration, Mothers day celebrations etc. where the cultural values and the genius of the people are meant to be remarkably manifested. First and foremost, it needs to be born in mind that Africans in general love to celebrate and they devote time meaningfully to worship God. One would therefore expect that the issue of the time or duration will not be in question. Africans have time for God. When it is time for worship the issue of time counts secondary if at all it is be considered.

2.  The kind of inculturated liturgy to be celebrated must be clear in one's mind. The liturgical celebration should never be reduced to a practising ground or rehearsal ground. The liturgy must be well thought out, the format must be simple to follow, the liturgical texts must be very well composed exhibiting well reflected ideas from the readings, the mystery that is being celebrated and couched in a manner that manifests the literal genre of a local church and the genius of the people.

3.  An inculturated eucharistic liturgy has to be a comprehensive rite, which necessarily must take care of the spiritual and emotional aspects of the people concerned through ample and rich musical embellishments, the sacral rhetorical, and liturgico-theological dimensions. The special areas where serious inculturation should be very remarkable are the following: new formularies for *the rite of breaking kola nuts, collects, prayer over the gifts, preface, prayer of con-*

*secration, prayer after communion and solemn prayer over the people, perhaps in the form of igo-ofo* – the litanic form of prayer of blessings peculiar to *Ndigbo*. Inculturated eucharistic celebration entails the product of intensive creative and innovative study as the matter cannot afford to be haphazard.

4.  Who are the participants? Are there people from other linguistic groups? Care must be taken that they are identified and made welcome and be fully integrated into the celebration. For in the liturgical assembly no one should be alienated. In God's house all are received as a fellow brother and sister in the common fatherhood of God. An aspect of this has to be demonstrated during the welcoming ceremony where such people should be recognised as much as possible by at least welcoming them in their language. This gesture disposes everyone and as such it will be possible to carry everyone along throughout the celebration.

5.  Accommodation for all should be assured: the clergy, the religious, the laity and liturgical functionaries in their various groups.[115]

6.  Proper thoroughfare will be need to facilitate free movement during celebration.

7.  The presence of a functional microphone cannot be over emphasised. The assembly has an inalienable right to hear whatever is being said clearly and distinctly.

8.  A live band can always be considered a great asset. Such a band will not only give the celebration a boom but also a boon. However, locally instrumented music would be preferable and should not be done without. Punctuality on the part of all especially the technicians and the band adds to the beauty of the celebration.

9.  All the liturgical ministers have to put in the best in them as they are equipped with their proper tools for maximum performance during the celebration:

    i.    the *celebrant* using the Altar Missal not Missalets or bulletins;
    ii.   the *deacon* with the book of the Gospel – the *Evangelia*;
    iii.  the *lectors* with the lectionary,
    iv.   the *cantors* with their proper book of songs for the responsorial psalm, alleluia verse etc;

v.   the *choir* with their proper musical texts and instruments,

vi.  the *acolytes* in the best form,

vii. the *ministers of hospitality* (the ushers[116] are being addressed in some places today in Europe and America), at their optimal performance and

viii. the *master of ceremonies* being alive to his duties,

ix.  the *technical crew* will be required to ensure an uninterrupted energy supply, and the microphones are well positioned at their appropriate places: on the altar, on the ambo, at the presidential seat, with the choir their excellent performance.

10.  The Sacristan ensures that all the necessary vessels, linens, the hosts, wine, water etc. are all in sufficient supply and are made available as and when due.

11.  The scene is a concelebrated eucharistic celebration involving the clergy with the bishop as the principal celebrant, the religious and the laity, as the case may be.

12.  The logical consequence for the proper execution of this proposed celebration will be the creation of an experiment centre or parish duly constituted. Having set the place in order, the following format is hereby proposed.


## The Invocation of the Holy Spirit and Other Choruses

At Mass or the Lord's Supper, the people of God are called together into unity, with the priest presiding and acting in the person of Christ, to celebrate the memorial of the Lord or Eucharistic sacrifice.[117] The role of the Holy Spirit as one who gathers God's people together for the eucharistic re-enactment and to sing the praises of God comes immediately to focus. For as one who completes the work of Christ, the Holy Spirit ensures that the promise of Christ applies supremely to such a local gathering of the church: for where two or three come together in my name, there am I in their midst (Matt.18:20). The Eucharistic celebration is essentially a manifestation of the Spirit of the glorified Christ.[118] Through the Holy Spirit every liturgical action manifests and actualises the presence of Christ in which the memorial of the salvific mystery does not just become a simple pious remembrance but an *anamnesis* or a historical salvific remembrance. It belongs to the Holy Spirit to excite the people to respond to God's invitation even as they decide to come to the church and their eventual convergence from the four corners of the church.[119]

Apart from drawing the people together, it is the Spirit that even prays in the gathered assembly and through his unction, the celebration is initiated and effectively brought to a successful end.[120] In the course of the celebration, it is the Spirit of God *who* gingers the assembly into prayerful action; who really prays in the worshipping assembly; who really transforms the assembly into true worshippers, forming them into a praying community. The Holy Spirit transforms the elements of bread and wine into the Body and Blood of Christ, and the assembly to become more Christ-like.

The presence of the choir, local musical instruments, live band and hand clapping, selected choruses rendered with good voice-production and powerful functional microphone become an immense asset to execute beautifully the first part of the celebration. The effect of good music at this juncture is inestimable. It adds to the creation of a conducive atmosphere for worship. It assists in no small measure in shading-off the distractions the people came along with to the celebration from the noisy and distracting world. The rendering of the music has to be purposeful and should not degenerate into another noise, thus multiplying distractions which it is meant to curb.

## The Procession

A liturgical procession initiates the celebration. By its very nature, it is a prayerful match towards the altar of sacrifice. It could be seen as a typical dramatisation of the triumphant entry of Jesus into Jerusalem distinguished by jubilant hymns (cf. Mk. 11:1-10; Jn.12:12).

Historically, liturgical procession could be described as the Roman system of welcoming their king or emperor as he came to address his people. The retinue consisted of torch lights carried in procession, with the people standing as a mark of honour and reverence as the emperor entered into the assembly.[121]

This entry rite can be well integrated into the eucharistic celebration by the use of an organised cultural dance to usher in the procession. One would expect such a dance to be mild, dignified, royal, processional and rhythmic. It does not need to be solemn but certainly not wild.

The cultural music continues until the bishop enters into the Church or main arena, as the case may be. At this moment, the choir takes over with the proper motet at the bishop's Mass.

In case there are other bishops, the commentator could be introducing them as they ascend the altar in a subdued but audible tone. The importance of this recognition could go a long way to dispose the visitors among them for an optimal active participation (especially if they are visiting bishops from other parts of the country or continents, like the Association of Episcopal Conferences of Anglo-phone West Africa -AECAWA and Catholic Bishops Conference of Nigeria – CBCN).

## The Sign of the Cross

| Ukochukwu: | **N' aha Nna na Nwa na Muo-nso.** |
| Priest: | In the name of the Father and of the Son and of the Holy Spirit. |
| **Oha:** | **Amen** |
| Assembly: | Amen |

## Commentary

The celebrant begins the ceremony with the normal invocation of the Most Holy Trinity, the Sign of the Cross, which is a christian form of prayer and typical of every christian gathering. Through it christians especially Catholics re-affirm their belief in the three Persons in one God, the role of the Cross in their life and in the mystery about to be celebrated. The Eucharistic celebration thus becomes a repeat dramatisation of Christ's sacrifice on the Cross, now at the Altar though in an unbloody manner under the appearance of bread and wine. When christians then gather to celebrate the Eucharist, they are fulfilling the Lord's command, *Do this in memory of me* (cf. Mk. 14:22-26; Lk.22:14-20; 1Cor.11:23-25). They recall the Lord's presence in their midst, for he promises his Church of his presence whenever they gather in his name (cf. Matt. 18:20).

## Welcome Rite by the Chief Celebrant

The rite involves greeting the people in their own traditional format and in the vernacular.

### *Emume Nnabata* – Rite of Reception

*After the sign of the Cross, the officiating minister greets the people in the cultural way as follows:*

| | |
|---|---|
| **Ukochukwu:** | **Ndi be anyi, nnonu ooh!** |
| Priest: | My dear people, welcome! |
| **Oha:** | **ooh!** |
| Assembly: | ooh! |
| **Ukochukwu:** | **Ndi be anyi, mma mmanu ooh!** |
| Priest: | My people, may it all be well with you |
| **Oha:** | **ooh!** |
| *Assembly:* | *ooh!* |
| **Ukochukwu:** | **Ndu nwoke! ndu nwanyi!** |
| Priest: | Life to all, men, women and children! |
| **Oha:** | **Iseeh!** |
| Assembly: | Amen! |
| | |
| **Ukochukwu:** | **Unu ga a-di, kaa nka!** |
| Priest: | May you live till old age |
| Oha: | Iseeh! |
| **Assembly:** | **Amen!** |
| | |
| **Ukochukwu:** | **Unu a-nwuchula!** |
| Priest: | May sudden and premature death not come to you! |
| **Oha:** | **Iseeh!** |
| Assembly: | Amen! |

| Ukochukwu: | **Ohaneze, ihe oma! ihe oma!** |
| Priest: | Good fortune to all present! |
| **Oha:** | **Iseeh!** |
| **Assembly:** | **Amen!** |

## Commentary

Among *Ndigbo*, in any formal gathering such as this, guests are formally greeted and welcomed by the host. The series of greetings portray the typical traditional way of greeting people when they gather for any formal function, the climax of which is the wish of life. For *Ndigbo*, life is very sacred in their belief, such that everything is centred around life. The people show their deep appreciation for life by the way they respect it and preserve it from any possible dangers. An Igbo proverb says: *Ndu bu isi* Life is primary. The greeting *May you live – I ga adi*, is about the best wishful greeting one can receive from another. So to wish someone not just life, but long life, free from sudden death, is the summary of all greetings. From this life then, one can cherish the life in abundance brought by Jesus Christ (cf. Jn 10:10) *I have come to give life and to give it abundantly.*

## Kiss of Peace

The essence of kiss of peace at this juncture is to create self-awareness among participants. One needs to know who is beside one and with whom you are worshipping.

## Presentation and Breaking of Kola Nuts

A selected group of the members of the Catholic Women Organisation (CWO) would bring some fine kolanuts, hand them over to selected members of the Catholic Men Organisation (CMO) who would in turn present the nuts to the assembly. The basis for this is to express vividly within a specific context, the new form of Ecclesiology of the *Church as a Family of God*. The image of the family is thus dramatised by the involvement of women, men and the entire people of God with each performing a distinctive role as in a human natural family. A representative of the CMO, most preferably the oldest man, would say the grace over the nuts in the form of *Igo ofo*, enunciating the good things and wishes on the assembly

## Emume Iwa Oji – Rite of Blessing of Kolanuts

The ceremony of blessing, breaking and eating of kolanut follows the normal procedure within the locality. Among Ndigbo, the main features of the rite include, carrying the kola round to various people according to their towns and villages. Prayer is said over it in which the ancestors are invoked. After having broken (and eaten the kola) the church's minister in fulfilment of his role as the president of the assembly, if he deems it necessary, concludes with a prayer recalling and incorporating the intentions raised at the Igo ofo oji, especially making reference to the ancestors, summarising those thoughts and putting them into what suffices for the presidential opening prayer. The Collect has to be a new composition exhibiting cultural literary genre and expression.

# Commentary

Oji or kolanut is an edible fruit from a kolanut tree which usually has a savoury bitter taste. It is a dominant ritual symbol among many African communities. Its appearance in the socio-cultural and commercial life of the peoples of Africa attracted the attention of some early writers to Africa as well as explorers, colonial administrators, Christian missionaries, anthropologists and West African novelists.[122] Its socio-cultural use is also registered among the major ethnic groups in Nigeria,[123] and serves as a ritual element in Central and West African regions.[124]

It usually comes in various sizes. A single seed of kola nut contains different pieces ranging from two to five being held together by nature. The number of the pieces has a tremendous cultural significance. In some parts of Igboland, a kola-nut with two pieces signifies unity of two hearts, referring to those around who are about to eat the nut: *obi anyi bu otu.* Three pieces signify solidarity and co-operation which are exemplified in the cultural realities like the cooking tripod *Ekwu ite*, which has three stands: it takes three to form a family, stressing co-operation as a necessary requirement for the success of any family. Four pieces signify the four market days (*Eke, Oye, Afo*, and *Nkwo*) that make up the Igbo traditional week days and which stands for all inclusiveness.

Incidentally every child in Igboland is born on one of these days and thus takes its first name from the particular market day. The prefix *Nwa* or *Ok'/Oke* son, added to the particular market day applies to males often marking them out as the sons of, or males born on that day, thus *Nweke or Okeke* would mean in this context, a son of *Eke day* or born on *Eke* day; *Nwoye* or *Okoye* as son of or born on *Oye* day; *Nwafo* or *Okafor* as son of or born on *Afor* day; *Nwankwo* or *Okonkwo* as son of or born on Nkwo day.

For females, the prefix *Mgbo* to the market day means a daughter of or born on a particular market day: *Mgbeke; Mgboye; Mgbafor; Mgbonkwor*. There are very rare occasions where kolanut has five or six pieces. Even at that, its interpretation has positive signification of long life and prosperity for all present.

There is hardly any social gathering among *Ndigbo* without the presentation of Kolanut. Kolanut forms an essential part of the people's culture.

To break and eat kolanut together means in Igbo Religion and culture, a symbol of hearty welcome, formal reception, genuine acceptance, hospitality, unity, reconciliation, peace, mutual trust and to a very large extent, it establishes a covenant relationship between the participants. When a guest is invited to a feast or even any casual visitation of a friend to another friend, the first act of courtesy is to shake hands of welcome accompanied by the expression *Nnoo* for the generality of Igboland; *Alua* for Nsukka and parts of Delta Igbo areas; *Ijee* for Awgu area; *Tuushia* for Nkanu area etc.

The next act of courtesy is the presentation of kolanut. The host presents the nut and hands it over to the guests. In a mixed gathering, the procedure for carrying kolanut varies from place to place. The kola needs to pass through the representatives of towns and villages that are present. One among these people seated especially the eldest in the gathering, would be asked to pray over the kola in what is referred to as *igo ofo oji*, praying over the kolanut. A well feasted guest could judge his reception as poorly if kola nut did not feature in the course of the whole feasting ceremony. Kolanut is as important as that in the Igbo traditional society.

In any Igbo traditional gathering, prayer over the kolanuts highlights the aims for which the assembly is convened and accordingly prays for the success of the assembly. The contents of the prayer often show that *Ndigbo* maintain that the Great God must give his approval before any prayer or sacrifice becomes efficacious. In the prayer format, God's name must first be invoked and he is implored to bind the evil spirits, while the god is told that its own demands have been met by giving him the victim or victims. Furthermore, *Ndigbo* believe that the good spirits are really servants or friends of God as they help him to keep the human race going and protect it from the ravages of the evil ones, who are believed to be the enemies of God, though they are still under God.[125]

In Igbo traditional religion, prayer over the kola takes the pattern of the normal *igo ofo* which consists of four or six major parts:

i.     the invocation
ii.    the confession of faults
iii.   the petition
iv.    blessings and curses
v.     thanksgiving and
vi.    sacred communion.[126]

By invoking God first in the prayer, one declares the supreme and pre-eminent position of God in the hierarchy of Igbo pantheon. He is the Great God – *Chukwu,* the King who lives in the sky: *Eze bi n' igwe,* Observer of all things both open and secret: *I na ahu n' ihe na a-hukwa na nzizo,* etc. Then after Him, are the other deities and ancestors.

In the prayer of confession, one acknowledges the frail nature of human beings, and the need to reconcile with God for an effective prayer. The belief that to err is human and to forgive is divine, *mmehie adighi mgbaghara ama di* is very much deeply rooted in the Igbo traditional religion. Offences are accordingly confessed as they relate to God and to fellow human beings.

## The Rite of Kola Nut As A Pre-Eucharistic Celebration for Ndigbo

The rite of kolanuts consists of their presentation, praying over them, breaking and eating them. In relation to the eucharistic celebration in the context of the Church as a family of God, one would expect some women of the congregation to provide the kolanuts. These will be handed over to some men of the congregation who then through their spokesman, announces loudly the arrival of the kolanuts. By presenting the kolanuts, the assembly feels welcomed and treated *humano modo.* The gesture thus helps to give God and the celebration a human face and makes liturgical attendance a visit to a friend and less an obligation. The Kolanuts personalise relationship through hospitality.[127] Since moderation is the norm of all virtues, the kola may not travel as far as it is supposed to, only a simply gesture of this could suffice.

Who does the blessing of the Kolanuts. The oldest man present could be asked to bless the kola on behalf of all present, or the priest who is functionally an elder or the bishop who is also known as the high priest – *nnukwu ukochukwu.*

Given the nature and the symbolism of this essential element in Igbo traditional society, locating the rite as part of the reception rite looks most reasonable. To situate it at the beginning tallies with the traditional rite of reception. It seals the welcoming ceremony of guests

Its function at this point ranges from welcoming the guests, creating the community of participants and ensuring a favourable atmosphere necessary for the celebration. It, furthermore, establishes the cordial rapport and mutual trust between members of the assembly as well as articulates the intentions for the assembly. Consequently, given the all familiar nature of the Kolanut rite, the assembly will easily understand the message of the celebration mediated through the kolanut. Nobody needs to teach anyone that they are all welcomed in the celebration at the beginning of which they have been served kolanut.[128]

The prayer over the kola aims at invoking God as the Supreme Being stressing at the same time the subordinate position of other deities and ancestors. It highlights the fact of pleading for forgiveness of sins, offences, faults, human frailties and imperfections – *njo, mmehie, na adighi ike nke madu.* It includes reconciliation and peace between oneself and God and with one another.

The emergent issues from the rite of kolanut in the celebration include the following:

i.     What is its role in relation to the penitential rite of the eucharistic celebration?

ii.    What is its role in relation to the opening presidential prayer, called the

iii.   collect?

iv.    What happens to the kola nuts after praying over it? To eat it or keep it till

v.     later especially with regard to the one hour pre-eucharistic fast?

With regard to the role of the rite of kola nut in relation to the penitential rite of the eucharistic celebration, opinions differ a great deal. Some are of the opinion that the penitential part of the Mass should not be omitted. It should be inserted somewhere in the rite because of its purificatory role in the Eucharist. Some are of the opinion that the penitential character in the rite may not be sufficiently Christian as to substitute for the penitential rite of the Mass. However, the emergent theological reason would be to have the prayers over the kola as a substitute for the penitential rite because of the sufficient contrite and ritual purification contained in the symbolism of breaking kolanut. Secondly, substituting it for the penitential rite removes the chances for duplication which the liturgy generally abhors. Thirdly, given the essence of authentic liturgical inculturation (authentic liturgical inculturation means doing it the people's way provided it is not essentially evil) it becomes rather obvious to substitute the foreign penitential rite of the Eucharist with a more culturally eloquent rite thus leading to the enhancement of the existing African Eucharist?

In relation to the presidential prayer, the same emergent theological reason holds that the prayer of the priest over the kola suffices as the opening prayer or collect, as the collect is essentially the summing up of the various articulated intentions of the assembly.

As to whether the kolanuts should be eaten or not, the innovation has been hotly debated and divergent opinions raised. Out of about ninety five opinions that were sought, about 15% were vehemently opposed to eating kolanut before the eating of the eucharistic meal. They based their arguments on the tradition of eucharistic fast before reception of the holy communion. About 25% sounded indecisive. A good number of about 58% spoke in favour of presenting, blessing, breaking and eating the kola nut within the eucharistic celebration and on special occasions in the church's liturgical year.

Confronted with the argument on the contrary, the argument in favour developed along the following line: If inculturation means anything, it means being faithful to the authentic cultural values and genius of the people which are not contrary to the faith.

With regard to the pre-eucharistic fast, the argument insists that one needs to distinguish clearly between law and love. If anything is born out of law, it then becomes legalism which has no room in the liturgy and, secondly, legalism especially in worship is the very thing Christ condemned. Whatever on the contrary is borne out of love, it is of Christ, for that is his mission on earth as well as the church's mission.

Furthermore, the very symbolism of Kolanut as an outward expression of hearty welcome, (*Tuushia, Nnoo*) togetherness, solidarity, unity, reconciliation, pardon, really falls in line with what the Eucharist stands for. Eating kolanut on a special occasion as this within eucharistic celebration should not be seen as diminishing reverence to the Eucharist, but rather as enhancing it and acting as a prelude or foretaste of what is to be fully realised later in the celebration of the Eucharist. The eating of kolanut in this case is a source of unity, unlike the early Christian's agape meal before the actual meal which degenerated into a source of division of the assembly. And St. Paul had to grapple with that problem as seen in 1Cor.11:17-25.

Here it will be important to recall briefly the history of the eucharistic fast. The fast came so that God's poor may not be embarrassed any more by the insensitive rich brother who gets drunk at the eucharistic meal while his brother goes home with empty stomach. It would be ironical if the fast is posited to foil a move to give back to the alienated brethren a sense of welcome to the Father's table. Perhaps, the handling of the problem of the eucharistic fast and the eating of kolanut will be the acid test of the Church's commitment to the will of God, so caring and also so terrible that it drew the whole blood of the only begotten Son for the sake of the adopted sons and daughters. One hopes that the response to eating kolanut within eucharistic celebration and for its symbolism for the people be dictated not by what people are used to but by what the heavenly Father wants.[129]

Suffice it say that the eating of the Kolanuts takes place within the eucharistic celebration and not outside of it or before it. So everything wholesome that happens within this celebration forms part of the eucharistic celebration itself and promotes it.

## Liturgy of the Word

The three readings are taken as usual. The first reading is taken from the Old Testament followed by the responsorial psalm. The responsorial psalm should be rendered in a harmonised musical form by three or four psalmists bringing out the four parts of a musical piece. It ought to be simple for the assembly to comprehend and participate in very easily. The second reading is taken from the New Testament, with the Alleluia verse, and the third, the gospel, is proclaimed by the deacon and followed by the homily to be given by a cleric as liturgical law stipulates.

The rediscovery of the power of the Word of God since the reforms of the Second Vatican Council has made a very powerful impact on the

Roman Catholic celebrations in Africa. Before the reforms of the Second Vatican Council, the use of the Bible was associated with Protestant worship, as recitation of the Rosary was with the Roman Catholic worship. But since after the reforms of the Council, the love for the Word of God among Africans was predictably extended to the Jewish-Christian Scriptures in African celebrations. For in Africa the word is everything, it cuts, it flays; it models, it modulates; it perturbs, it maddens; it heals or kills; it amplifies or lowers according to its force; it excites or calms souls.

The Word of God is effective, indictive and provocative. It can excite into a response. It is challenging and dynamic. It elicits sorrow for sins. it convinces one of guilt. It arouses a feeling of repentance, conversion, remedial action and resolution. It produces remorse for one's past actions and leads to a true purpose of amendment. It gives hope in a hopeless situation. It assures one of God's love and readiness to accept the offender back. It gives courage for a new and decisive beginning.

In the celebration of the Word, one needs to draw attention to the recognition of the power of the Word in the liturgy. The Word is the sacred (mystical) patrimony of the community. The Word is too large for the mouth of an individual to pronounce, because it belongs to God. It requires the mandate of the community for an individual to proclaim it.

Against this backdrop, it would be very proper that the readers of the first and second readings, and the psalmists, come before the principal celebrant and receive the people's mandate by asking for blessing, almost as deacons and priests do for the proclamation of the Gospel when a bishop is the principal celebrant.

*As the three come before the principal celebrant, one or the three ask for blessing saying: **I/we believe in the Word of God and I/we ask you to bless me/us so that I/we may proclaim it with faith.***
Priest says:
**May the almighty God who sends you to proclaim His Word of salvation to His people, bless you and open your eyes and your lips to proclaim His Word with sincerity.**
**Reader/Readers answer:**      **Amen.**

The potency and efficacy in the well proclaimed Word of God can never be over-emphasised. There is life in the Word: ***The Word took flesh***

***and dwelt among us*** (cf. Jn.1:14). As a pastoral strategy the proclamation of the Word and the preaching of the Word could be preceded by some praise songs. It is a means of softening the soil of the human heart for the sowing of the Word of God.

## Gloria

Having been purified, the assembly feels ritually cleansed to join their voices with those of the angels to sing: Glory to God in the highest, and peace to men on earth who are God's friends. Here the rendering in the vernacular expresses the point much clearer, *Otito diri Chukwu n'enu kasi enu, n'uwa udo diri ndi madu, ndi ihe ha na-aso Chukwu.* The joyful song of the angels at the birth of Christ challenges the assembly to a very high moral rectitude.

Any other suitable alternative would also suffice like Glory be to God in the Highest, with Alleluia as response. The *Gloria* or its equivalent should never be recited especially on a Sunday any more than anyone would recite the song, *Happy Birthday to you* at a birthday party. Besides, it is only used in a context of great solemnity. [130]

## Prayer of the Faithful

The prayer of the faithful is to be very well adapted to the needs of the universal and local Church and the sentiments of the people at public worship. Possibly calling people to pray spontaneously on specific intentions usually for the Church and her ministers, for the country, for all present, for the needy, and for the departed appears most practical.

Each of these intentions could be accompanied by a proper singing response for instance, for the dead, the response could read, *Meghee onu uzo, onu uzo nke enuigwe, meghee onu uzo, ka umunne anyi bata:* Open the gate, open the gate of heaven, that our departed brothers and sisters may enter. After the five intentions, the celebrant could invite the assembly if time allows, to a private prayer for their special intentions for which they came for the celebration.

After some reasonable moment of silent prayer, the celebrant sums up the prayer by either invoking the Blessed Virgin Mary with Hail Mary, or singing some parts of her litany or any popular Marian hymn and then concludes. This kind of praying format if well organised, is gradually replacing the stereo-typed written intentions in the official liturgical book. Occasionally, this format should be used not only to serve as variety but also to serve as a kind of *editio typica*, a format or standard open to alteration.

## Offertory

The rite consists of bringing on of gifts of bread, wine (locally produced) water, other offerings in cash and kind carried by members of the assembly to the altar for sacrifice. This should be done as described above with all amount of pomp and pageantry, accompanied by musical instruments, singing, clapping and dancing to the altar of sacrifice.

## Eucharistic Prayer

This includes the prayer over the gifts, preface, prayer of consecration. In the light of authentic inculturated celebration, these should be new and original compositions as already said in the case of the Collect prayer. It means that for each special occasion a special composition should accompany it. As much as possible, the consecretory prayer could be adapted to the local dialogic African pattern of praying.

## Communion Rite

The Rite is to be celebrated in the spirit of African sense of commensality, eating together, sometimes referred to as *nliko nwanne na nwanne* – the act of eating and drinking together as blood related brothers and sisters. In this case no one is fed in the mouth as all are mature adults because it is only infants and sick adults that are fed in the mouth in public. The liturgy is essentially a public worship of Christ the Head and members. To feed an adult in the mouth publicly may be culturally obnoxious and unacceptable.

In some African set-ups, it is abhorrent for a man to feed a woman with bread in the mouth in public without the act being interpreted as solicitous. The nobility of the Church's liturgy disallows the introduction of whatever culture frowns at or abhors into her worshipping forms.

In this case, it may be better to present the *ciborium* for people to take. The sense of *he gave* will still be respected without doing any harm to a wholesome cultural value and the mystery being celebrated from being odious to the people. The moral purity of the participants would still be demanded. In other words it would not become a free for all kind of food. For even in the cultural setting, one needs to accord food some degree of respect and dignity. Just as one cannot return from the farm and join in the family meal table without first having to tidy oneself up by washing ones hands at least, so should all participants treat themselves to a true ritual cleansing before participating worthily at the Eucharistic banquet.

## The Creed

Without prejudice to the fact that the profession of faith is to express the assent and response of the people to the Scripture reading and homily they have just heard, and to recall to them the main truths of the faith, before they begin to celebrate the Eucharist,[131] the creed could be given an extended meaning by way of its location at this point. The initial restricted significance can be prolonged to be professed after Communion. At this juncture, the two integral parts of the Eucharist have been celebrated, the Creed thus, more meaningfully expresses the assent and response of the people not only to the Scripture readings and homily but also to the Eucharist just received. At this juncture, the entire Eucharist celebrated is seen as an integral faith and not dichotomised one. The Creed becomes an affirmation of the oneness of the faith not on one aspect but on the two aspects of the Eucharist.

Furthermore, the Creed is not strictly a prayer. It serves to remind the assembly of the cardinal tenets of their religion, which they ought to remember always. The Sunday eucharistic celebration becomes a privileged locus to satisfy this need. What is said about Gloria by way of rendering it applies also to the Creed, although sometimes recitation appears more practical and meaningful.

It needs to be added that it can be recited in the place of post communion meditation and worship song especially on Sundays and Solemnities.[132] Otherwise, the post meditation and worship songs take place at this juncture.

The Creed, it must be noted, has no fixed place in the eucharistic celebration. The recitation or singing of the Creed is rather secondary in the celebration. It is an element similar to the statues in cathedrals that can be moved or even taken away without endangering the solidity of the edifice. That is really what happens since the majority of the Masses do not have the Creed, and the equilibrium of the celebration is not threatened because of that, but rather improved.[133]


## Post Communion Prayer

As said above about Collect and Eucharistic Prayer, the post Communion prayer should be a new composition for each celebration.


## Dismissal

The Rite of dismissal has to be celebrated with a great sense of mission. It is meant to remind the assembly of their missionary role after having been fed with the Word and Sacrament. The rite is meant to challenge the assembly to act as leaven of the society; to draw agenda for social justice based on the paschal mystery just celebrated for the gradual but steady transformation of the world through charity or sacrificial love.

Ordinarily at the end of any formal gathering, people wish each other good bye with some gestures like handshake. The assembly could easily wish each other good bye with a handshake accompanied by a greeting such as: *God loves you! May you have a blessed new week* etc. The gesture is to internalise and personalise the entire celebration in a human way of life. The exit hymn thus follows hereafter.

# CHAPTER FOUR

## ANNOUNCEMENTS AND EXTRA COLLECTIONS

## Introduction

The tendency towards long announcements at the eucharistic worship has the double danger of derailing and overburdening the liturgy. Worse still is a situation of long announcements and other numerous extra collections apart from the normal offering. There seems to be a growing tendency to over-load the eucharistic celebration with these and some other activities no matter how important they may appear. Granted that in the missions the church is still at the basic developmental stage, the church in this case needs funds to carry out not only the infra structural needs but also the running costs of maintaining the church, the ministers and other attendant financial problems, prudence however, should be the norm in this regard. The church in the missions must struggle to survive and find her feet firmly on the ground so that having been well established, it could supply help to places in need, but not at the detriment of the very *raison d'être* of the church, namely the eucharistic celebration.

However reasonable these motives may be, must the eucharistic celebration be reduced to what it is today on account of long announcements and second to fourth collections as the case may be? The Eucharistic celebration has become a means and a forum for fund raising in view of the many legitimate needs of the parish or diocese such that the danger of losing the message of the mystery just celebrated is obvious.

With regard to announcements, they have sometimes become very nauseating such that some people would sadly leave the church without the closing rite of the celebration especially the final blessings. As a remote cause of this anomaly, the eucharistic celebration is thus reduced to a kind of buffet, where one comes to pick and choose. One stays up until after communion and abandons the later part as a matter of choice. Such a dichotomy militates against the celebration.

Not only that some of these announcements are absolutely unnecessary, they are sometimes being *preached* instead of being *made* thereby making it still much longer. Sometimes, they are deliberately *repeated*. At first by the announcer and secondly by the priest with the intention of emphasising some of the points.

Sometimes, ministers of the Word have either been cautioned or warned to cut the homily very short between five to ten minutes to allow for thirty to forty minutes announcements. By way of proportion therefore, the time allotted to announcements would be more than that of the homily.

Of course immediately after the so called short homily the rest of the celebration is hurried, resulting in over use of the second eucharistic prayer which features every day in the weekday masses and then on Sundays. The result is the neglect of other eucharistic prayers because they are considered too long. Variety which is the spice of life is now sacrificed on the altar of long announcements and numerous collections.[134]

Another danger involved in long announcements is the tendency even to forget the Readings of the day and the little message one is able to catch during the brief homily. In effect, announcements defeat the purpose of the liturgy of the Word, which is an integral part of the eucharistic celebration. On account of this misplacement of values, there is the tendency for the people to leave the celebration with the announcements other than the actual message of the celebration. There is also that tendency to forget the first announcements at the end of the long list.

With regard to extra-offerings, the situation is about the same. The so-called Father's offering refers to the first offering of bread and wine and the cash and kind offerings that go along simultaneously. This offering is often very modestly carried out with the normal motets from the parish choir as the case may be. Often the hymns are deeply theological, referring to the offerings of Christ on the altar of the Cross, whose memorial the church re-enacts in the celebration. Some refer to this offering as the Eucharistic offering.

Shortly after this, are the others. There could be two or three in a row with catchy names attached to each. For instance, monthly Project Sunday collection, Parish Workers Salary collection Sunday, My name is in the book collection Sunday, etc. This row of collections will be conducted in a different musical atmosphere from the first. It ranges from choruses to live band performance so that the yield would be maximal. These could then drag on and on amidst dancing and clapping in the name of the Lord. Some parishes hold these collections immediately after the Father's offering, while some locate it after communion. In either case, it is usually long. Those who locate it after the first one seem to have some little advantage because no one would likely leave the church before communion. Those who locate theirs after communion may not be as lucky as the first. Because, like what obtains at the announcements whereby some people out of annoyance leave the church, they also leave before the long collections. How long shall these rather alienating practices in the eucharistic celebration continue?

The most subtle aspect of these collections stems from the new attitude of most people. Someone comes to church with twenty Naira (in the Nigeria context) for instance, meant for the offertory. This sum is to be given ordinarily at the offertory as has been ear-marked. So instead of dropping it once and for all, may be at the first collection, one changes it into four places, giving of course five Naira for each and, therefore, dancing to the altar four times. So whether one gives it at once where there is only one offertory or four times where there are four offertories, the over all result is the same. One does not rule out those who could give more as often as the collections are called. But the percentage does not seem to be much. How long shall this unholy wisdom of self-deception continue in the celebration of the Eucharist. The church needs announcements and funds but is it at all costs? or at the detriment of her *raison d'être*?

## Nature of Eucharistic Liturgy

It may be necessary to recall that the eucharistic celebration has got a beauty and shape by which it is characterised. The eucharistic celebration is the centre of the christian community;[135] the source and summit of the christian life;[136] the centre and culmination of the entire life of the christian community.[137] The eucharistic celebration remains the locus *par-excellence* where the gathered community meets Jesus Christ, present in his Word, present in the Eucharist, and present in the celebrating community.[138] The privileged presence of Christ in the eucharistic celebration recognises the other ways in which he is present which cannot be equalled to the degree of his presence in the eucharistic celebration.

Two thousand years have clothed this celebration with a cloak of many splendours. Within all those years it has also accumulated layers of dust and introduced practices which, through continual use, have assumed the mask of principles. If the apostles were to attend one of our Masses today, they would have great difficulty recognising the Paschal meal that they celebrated with Jesus in the Upper Room.[139] Although one cannot exactly say how much time Christ and the apostles spent in celebrating the first Eucharist, it could well be said that the celebration in the Upper Room was very much distinguished by simplicity, brevity, sobriety and practicality.

## Eucharistic Liturgy in the Primitive Church

The earliest account of how the eucharistic liturgy was conducted came from Justin, Martyr,[140] a convinced christian and philosopher who would not compromise his beliefs, but rather cried his faith aloud. It was in the course of proclaiming his faith that he gave to posterity one of his most beautiful treatises on the celebration of the Eucharist, and the celebration of the Lord's Day.

He first called the celebration, the liturgy of the Lord's Day. He referred to the assembly as a community of love and prayer. According to him, those who have any resources come to the aid of all who are in need, and we are always assisting one another. For all that we eat we thank the Maker of the universe through his Son Jesus Christ and the Holy Spirit.

With regard to the celebration of the Lord's Day he noted: On the day named after the sun,[141] all who live in the city or countryside assemble. The memoirs of the apostles or the writings of the prophets are read for as long as time allows.[142]

When the lector has finished, the president addresses us and exhorts us to imitate the splendid things we have heard. Then we all stand and pray.[143] When we have finished praying, bread, wine and water are brought up. The president then prays and gives thanks according to his ability[144] and the people give their assent with an Amen! Next, the gifts over which the thanksgiving has been spoken are distributed, and everyone shares in them, while they are also sent via the deacons to the absent brethren.

The wealthy who are willing make contributions, each as he pleases, and the collection is deposited with the president, who aids orphans and widows, those who are in want because of sickness or some other reason, those in prison and visiting strangers. In short, he takes care of all in need.

He further described the day thus: It is on Sunday that we all assemble, because Sunday is the first day: the day on which God transformed darkness and matter and created the world, and the day on which Jesus Christ our Saviour rose from the dead. He was crucified on the eve of Saturn's day[145] and on the day after, that is on the day of the sun, he appeared to his apostles and disciples and taught them what we have now offered for your examination.[146]

From the account of Justin, there is evidence of two offerings: the offering of bread, wine and water that takes place after the liturgy of the Word; the second offering that takes place after communion in the form of offering in cash. From the proceeds of this second collection the primitive church was able to cater for the genuine needs of the community. There is no evidence of any other extra collection within the eucharistic celebration. These two offerings in Justin's account, the church combines today into one during the first offering time after the liturgy of the Word.

Be that as it may, suffice it to note that one is dealing with tendencies and the consequent abuses. Granted that the early church did what they did to cater for the immediate needs of their members, today more than ever, there are changing needs and situations. The advantage of history is to create awareness of what happened in the past, to show us pit-holes to avoid and to improve on the *status quo*.

# Sunday: The Day of the Lord and of the People

## As The Day of the Lord

Sunday, the day of the sun as mentioned by Justin, is regarded as the day of the Lord, in which all in a given locality gather for prayers, to listen to the Word and to celebrate the Eucharist. It is indeed the day which the Lord has made, in which we have to rejoice and be glad *(cf. Ps. 118:24). It is held holy because of the resurrection which is the bed rock of the Christian faith. It is the day of the new creation by God.*

The Sunday celebration of the Lord's Day and his Eucharist is at the heart of the church's life.[147] The Sunday Eucharist is the foundation and confirmation of all christian practices.[148] Participation in the communal celebration of the Sunday Eucharist is a testimony of belonging and of being faithful to Christ and to his church.[149] All these combine to accord Sunday the dignity it enjoys in the catholic faith and this has been observed all through the centuries to the present day. It needs to be noted that such is a wholesome tradition that should be encouraged and enriched with the values of the people in order to save it from being a mere routine. Instead it should be observed as a day of joyful celebration and celebrated accordingly.

## As the Day of the People

Another important aspect of Sunday is that it is the day in which people assemble, a day in which people cease from work to rest in order to accord the day the dignity and importance it deserves. It is a day of grace and rest from work. Just as God rested on the seventh day from all his work, human life has a rhythm of work and rest. The institution of the Lord's Day helps everyone to enjoy adequate rest and leisure, to cultivate their familial, cultural, social and religious lives.[150]

For all christians, like the early christians of Africa who were often brought before the court to explain why they gathered on Sundays, who would often respond thus: our Christianity has no meaning without the celebration of Sunday. It is the day of the Lord, the day of the resurrection and the day of the Eucharist. The present day and its tendency to equiprate Sunday and weekend should be reviewed in the light of the theological basis of observing Sunday as a work free day, and a day of rest.

Sunday rest means more than abstention from work in order to clear the arrears of sleep which have been incurred as a result of early rising to go to work during the weekdays. It means more than weekend whereby one can engage in long travels or attend to other social demands as the main purpose. Nor is it reducible to that free period in which one recuperates from the fatigue of daily work in order to feel strong to face the hectic demands of the following week.

Sunday marks rather, the beginning of a new week. The nature of Sunday has to do with life. It forms the source of christian life and nourishment of the same life. Life does not begin with work. Life exists before work. One works to live but does not live to work. Life is a gift, it is not earned. Life is not reducible to work and money and what money can buy. Work and money accruing from it is not everything. There are situations in life when even money can fail. There are other values more than work and money. Such values include, having quality time for God and for others. This is the theologico-social character of Sunday that needs to be emphasised in our liturgical catechesis. In other words, over and above every other purpose of Sunday, it should be a day for the Lord, a day reserved exclusively for God after which other social, familial and cultural values could be addressed.


## Announcements That Weaken The Eucharistic Liturgy

One refers here to two kinds of announcements, namely, some unnecessary announcements and long announcements. Some announcements appear in such a manner that one begins to wonder really their relevance in the eucharistic celebration. The situation becomes even more complex when they are ill timed. For instance, the celebrant has just introduced the celebration and thus sets the pace and tempo of the Mass. Then comes a long list of those who have booked for the Mass, for example, an anonymous person wishes to pray for thanksgiving and God's protection. If someone chooses to be anonymous it is understandable that his or her intention should equally be anonymous. Such an announcement should not be made because of the anonymity. Then at the end of it all, the announcer says: to these you may add your own private intentions. It is not intended by so saying that the names of donors for Masses should not be announced, the issue is the timing, the place, the length and the reasonableness.

It needs to be recalled that the list is an essential part of the eucharistic celebration. Common sense recommends that the list of those requesting for Mass be called much earlier before the Mass starts. Depending on the length of the list, it could start fifteen to twenty minutes time and finish earlier enough for the entrance hymn or processional hymn to start.

The homilist barely ends a preaching on a very high challenging note, and the congregation is having a quiet time to digest the Word of God proclaimed in the readings and the homily given by the preacher, and then comes an announcement saying: *Please may the owner of the car with the registration number, go and remove it from its present stand for it is blocking the flow of traffic. Or may the owner of such a vehicle go and put off the head light or the parking light.* Surely, no one would like to come out of a celebration and have a run down battery. But the good intended to achieve militates against the general good through the distraction and disruption of the mystery being celebrated?

In most cases, the celebrant spends sixty to ninety minutes to celebrate the entire Mass, the announcer takes thirty to forty five minutes to announce banns of marriage, diocesan meetings, parish meetings, society meetings including those who have their specific days in the week for their get together, those to sweep the church next Saturday, the result of the previous weeks second or special collection according to zones which may be ranging from ten to more zones accompanied with clapping and commentaries that go with such announcements. After the announcer, then as the case may be, the priest or the celebrant or the parish priest takes his own time supposing by so doing to stress further almost all the points raised by the last speaker. The tendency is that often all the major issues raised in the readings, the homily and prayers of the celebration are suffocated by these unliturgical announcements. The risk is that the congregation goes home, without much spiritual enrichment and nourishment.

Do we by saying this suggest the abolishing of all kinds of announcements in our eucharistic celebrations. By no means. But the present situation of the place of announcements needs to be reviewed in favour of the eucharistic mystery.

## Reasons Advanced to Justify the Long Announcements

The ordinary reason often given to justify the long announcements is the fact that majority of the members of the assembly are illiterate. Their inability to read and write necessitates writing everything out and reading them out verbatim. This argument goes but not too far. Personal experiences show that even in some Mass centres and chaplaincies in tertiary institutions, where it is evident that more than ninety nine percent are more than literate, the same experience of long announcements still takes place although in lesser degree than in an ordinary parish set up. Again the argument insists that for the sake of the minority there is no way out.

Another reason being advanced in favour of long announcements maintains that the people need to be reminded of even the things they know already since human beings are prone to forget. Plausible as this may sound, it needs to be observed that even to remind people, when the reminding list becomes endless, people have also the tendency to forget the first set of issues by the time one finishes. And one comes back to square one. Thirdly, one argues that in some cases some announcements need to be duplicated. The first announcement of some matters may not suffice until they are repeated with renewed emphasis at the second time. Wasting words can never be a virtue on this special occasion.

Most seriously, there appears a lurking exhibition of amateur oratory on the part of some announcers. Some see the announcements as their own turn to address the assembly. Therefore, every display of oratory must come into play. This often shows itself in preaching the announcements instead of dropping them and giving unnecessary details. This tendency if not properly and timely checked could reduce the celebration to a mere talkative liturgy.

# Criteria for Matters for Announcements

Recognising the dignity of the mystery being celebrated, definitely not every item qualifies for announcement. The issue must be directly connected with the on-going celebration, affecting the majority of the assembly, and must be very urgent and seen to be so otherwise a great harm may be caused.

Just as people go around discovering cars parked with lights on, people should be detailed to direct traffic in the parking lot. As people park, the traffic wardens should forestall the announcement by seeing that drivers park properly and as they direct the drivers, they should have special eye on the light to see that they are all put off before the driver leaves the car. Drivers should particularly check their lights before leaving their cars for worship. For when such announcements about light are made, the congregation is distracted, in addition to the embarrassment it causes all those who know about the cars in question. Of course, in parking such cars, the wardens should maintain that the thoroughfare is left free for easy flow of traffic.

Where and when the announcements like the intentions, banns and meetings must of necessity be made, one should consider making them briefly at the beginning of the celebration. The amount of time it usually takes to make the announcements should be anticipated before the fixed time for the Mass to begin. In effect, if the Mass is to begin at six, announcements could begin at about five thirty or five forty, so that at six on the dot, the Mass begins. This saves time. The argument that all would not be there at the beginning to hear the announcements jeopardises the dignity of the celebration. The simple theological implication of this suggests that it would be better to miss the introductory part of the Mass and in some cases even to miss the liturgy of the Word, as people still come in after the homily than to miss the announcements, because after communion all should have been there.

On even a more serious note, the harm one anticipates in missing the announcements at the beginning cannot be compared to the blessing one loses when they are made at the end where people go without the blessings. It pays more to miss the announcements made at the beginning of the celebration than to miss the penitential part of the Mass and the liturgy of the Word as the case may be. The basic issue is that even if all are present at the beginning, it is still proper to hear the announcements so that once the celebration starts, there would be an unbroken continuation and the assembly could very easily experience the close nexus of the various units of the celebration.

Alternatively, let the announcements be made at exactly the time the celebration should have normally started, so that no one could be accused of either not hearing the announcements or causing others to be unreasonably late. This saves the celebration from being unnecessarily interrupted.

In other words, the Eucharistic celebration should flow uninterruptedly. If the dictum that *what one hears last, that is what one takes home*, holds true, let it be said that the assembly that has celebrated without any went home with the fruits of the mysteries for their own sanctification, edification and the glorification of God. Announcements can hardly achieve these noble objectives as enunciated in the documents on the sacred liturgy by the Fathers of the reformed liturgy of the Second Vatican Council.[151]

Such announcements in actual fact vitiate the active, conscious, plenary and socio-Communitarian participation in the Eucharistic celebration. Thus announcements against this background contradict the aims of the reformed liturgy which advocates maximum participation in the liturgical celebration.[152]

Such announcements breed boredom. They make the liturgical celebration unduly long especially when the announcer preaches the announcements instead of simply dropping the message. By so doing, it contravenes the spirit of the liturgy which opts that liturgical celebrations be distinguished by noble simplicity, noble brevity, noble sobriety and noble practicality.[153] Brevity they say is the soul of business. Boredom kills interest.

## Place of Other Collections in the Eucharistic Liturgy

These other collections should be seen and understood within the context of the Eucharistic celebration. Although the convention today places such collections after communion, perhaps recalling the practice of the early church even though wrongly, it needs to be seen in its proper perspective. Incidentally, offering time seems to be the moment where inculturation is very evident in some churches. Given the attitude of the people, it may be a matter of liturgical catechesis and perhaps simple common sense.

The liturgical catechesis consists of the fact the nature and meaning of any offering or collection at the eucharistic celebration must be clearly linked up with the celebration. It does not really matter the objective or how many of such extra offering. It needs to be noted that all gifts can only be properly offered during the Eucharistic celebration, and must be linked up with it. It must be seen as an extension of the eucharistic sacrifice with the aim of reaching out beyond the confines of the eucharistic arena. For it is only then that all gifts are transformed into Jesus through whom they now have infinite value before the Father.

Indeed, actual offering occurs during the eucharistic offering, and thus it becomes the gifts of the christian community which include bread, wine, water, and collections in cash and kind. Furthermore, the assembly offers all that it has and are: mind, soul and body and indeed, all it possesses. Actually, at the offertory, humanity expresses the willing response to God's offer of partnership in which humanity is invited to a magnanimous divine friendship. God invites humanity to a partnership with him in the cosmic enterprise of making the world beautiful through sacrificial love. At the offertory, humanity demonstrates the voluntary response of involvement in this partnership of sacrifice. Thus, all human gifts at offertory are given to the Lord, who will transform them through the action of the priest at consecration rendering them acceptable to the Father.

In making such an offering against this background, the assembly fulfils faithfully the mind of the Master. The assembly sees itself as faithful imitator and active participant in the offering of Christ. It sees meaning and relevance in what it celebrates.

Liturgical catechesis demands that such extra offerings should be seen and understood within the context of the on-going celebration. They should not be divorced from it. It becomes necessary that whatever financial need a particular church has will have to be integrated within the celebration. It would be very important to inform the people well ahead of time of the needs of the church and the importance of generosity. The practical effect of this understanding would be that the extra collections or offerings become unnecessary. Secondly, to meet the demanding needs of a particular assembly, a ratio or percentage system could be most advisable and recommendable. In effect, so much ratio or percentage for the priest and those he has to cater for weekly as mentioned by Justin, and so much for this and other projects.

Common sense will then instruct that many collections apart from the main offertory will become rather redundant since the same aim would be achieved by that one and only offertory. Secondly, that one offertory should be celebrated as elaborately as possible. Instead of the unnecessary dichotomy of the first and other collections, especially in the way they are conducted, the choir, the band and all should come into full play *to make the offering time not only the blessing time, but really a one- is -one affair.*

## Thanksgiving For Favours Received

In most parishes today, people have grown into the good habit of coming to give thanks to God for favours received. This is expressed in two common ways. It is first expressed by booking for Mass which they expect to be announced and celebrated in their presence most preferably on a Sunday. Second, as the Mass is being celebrated for this named intention, they come to the altar with gifts. The number of such thanksgiving offerings each Sunday varies from parish to parish. It is very remarkable most often in urban parishes and in the rural areas especially during the Christmas season when there is mass exodus from the urban to the rural areas.

No one frowns at this newly acquired spirit of generosity and viable means of supporting the church's ministers and the presbyteries. The one question that often arises in this regard is at what point in the Mass can this exercise best take place? Some people have noted some kind of abuses arising from this, like being rowdy, prolonging the Mass unduly.

Some have reported a certain sense of exhibitionist tendency. These are of the opinion that the thanksgiving offering should either take place after communion or privately for instance, by going quietly to the rectory's store or sacristy and deposit such items. In some places one hears of banning such offerings without any serious theological reason apart from saving time (without giving proper account of what one does with the time saved).

It may be proper to realise that as a mission land, dehydrated theological definitions and dry celebrations would not fully apply here especially within a culture that is exuberant in nature. Would it not be better to harness the overt generosity of the people by supporting them, encouraging them and linking up their thanksgiving with the eucharistic celebration.

Pastoral reasons may even dictate that, where people are given to generous thanksgiving of this nature, no matter their number, it should be encouraged to go on. One would expect such a Mass to be the last Mass of the morning session or of the day as the case may be. One would expect that the celebrant does not hurry the celebration, but maintains some moderation with regard to time and above all the dignity demanded for eucharistic celebration. People's sense of generosity should neither be injured nor sacrificed on the Altar of gaining time. Above all the sentiments of the people must be respected especially when it comes to worship and offering thanks to their God.

## Conclusion

Experience often shows that on account of long and unnecessary announcements and prolonged series of collections, the assembly comes out of the celebration with little or no joy on their faces. A typical cultural celebration proves the contrary. When people are returning from a cultural celebration certain degree of joy radiates on their lips and faces. Their voices recount as much as possible the highlights of the events that they have just witnessed. They re-tell the various aspects of the celebration that touched them most.

Think of the spectators after a successful football match for instance. As they come out of the playing ground en route the homes, it is all recalling the major events that took place during the match. Praises are showered where necessary and blames are apportioned accordingly. At least the content of the chat is reminiscent of the game which they have just been treated to.

The christian assembly comes out discussing anything other than the mystery just celebrated. They seem to be overburdened with confused mystery which is ordinarily mysterious and the long announcements and collections which combine to steal away the joy and re-telling of events of the celebration on their lips and faces.

Would it not therefore become imperative to restore the spirit of celebration in the worshipping community by insisting on celebrating the Paschal Mystery of Christ in one continuous frequency instead of overburdening the celebration with aliturgical issues? The Paschal Mystery which is the nerve-centre of the christian life must be allowed to effect the radical changes inherent in it, the result of which would naturally lead to generosity, true christian spirit of active response to the various needs of the church. The church must insist on seeking first the kingdom of God and its justice and all the other things will be added unto her (cf. Matt. 6:33).

Conscientious efforts should be made at all levels of each local church to give an aggressive approach to the shameful issue of illiteracy. When more than ninety percent are able to read and write, that could go a long way indeed to reduce the amount of time being hitherto spent on announcements. Suffice it to say that a thing is not convincing because it is repeated *(ad nauseam)* to a nauseating point, instead the adage that says that a word is enough for the wise cannot be faulted especially in this case.

The culture of visiting the parish notice boards to read up information needs to be cultivated. This applies to all especially the literate ones, until a time when the greater percentage would be able to read and write.

Efforts should not be spared to save the eucharistic liturgy from being a talkative worship which could be a small index of a big whole of turning Christianity into a talkative religion. Instead the eucharistic celebration should be distinguished by active participation, zero distraction, prayerful meditation, self-transformation, total sanctification of the whole assembly, edification of the Mystical Body of Christ giving rise to ultimate glorification of God. One should be able to say at the end of each celebration, thanks be to God, one has really been able to pray and encounter God.

Every collection made within the Eucharistic liturgy must be seen to be closely connected to the sacrifice and self offering of Christ which the Eucharist being celebrated re-enacts in a most excellent manner. Such collections should be done sparingly so that the people's sense of generosity will continue to be sustained leading to a maximum result each time. When it is too often, it loses the force and efficacy, for monotony says an adage, kills interest. Virtue they say stands in the middle – *virtus in medio stat* is yet another relevant saying. The Word of God and the Eucharist are responsible for the nourishment and growth of the people of God, the church. Nothing should dare to replace or jeopardise them.

Announcements should be done with utmost discretion. Let them be made where they affect either the generality of the assembly or at least a great majority. Extra collections are to be done where they are absolutely necessary. Let them be done in connection with the offerings of Christ, and not exceeding two offerings at any given time. This will save the act of offering from the theory of diminishing return.

# CHAPTER FIVE

# EVANGELISATION: AN ECCLESIAL TASK AT ALL LEVELS

## Introduction

Without Evangelisation the church lacks an essential dimension. The main thrust of Evangelisation *is to make Christ present, make him known and make him loveable.* Evangelisation can well be understood as a process by which a person is led to make a commitment to Christ and dedicate oneself to a Christ-like way of life. Thus, one becomes a vital member of the local church. Evangelisation entails a determined effort towards a continuous or an on-going conversion, authentic proclamation and exemplary witnessing to the risen Lord.

Evangelisation is not yet another programme in the church. It is definitely more than a programme. It is rather an essential component of any christian community. It is part and parcel of the church. It belongs to the church by its very being to evangelise. Through Evangelisation, the church transforms the entire community, nay, the human society. It demands, therefore, no programme but a vision instead.

The church has at the official level embraced Evangelisation whole-heartedly. The hierarchy of the church has clarified the themes of Evangelisation,[154] and the bishops in various parts of the world are giving Evangelisation a top priority in their areas of jurisdiction.[155]

It needs to be an essential and crucial part of the core christian experience. Every christian is baptised not only for him or herself but for others. The church in her members is to become the Gospel others hear and experience so that, by so witnessing, others may share the source of christian joy.[156]

# Evangelisation: A Practical Application of Theology

Just as Evangelisation is not yet another programme in the church but rather a part and parcel of the church's life and ministry, so also with the concept of evangelisation as a new theology as much as an application of theology. One needs to conceive evangelisation as a necessary component of every ministry in the church and a careful integration of theology into the various aspects of human endeavour.

It means bringing Christ to bear on all facets of life, christian, socio-economic, political, educational, developmental etc. Evangelisation aims at total transformation of the human person and society through proclamation, conversion and community according to Acts 2 in the spirit of Rev. 21: 5: which says, *behold I make all things new.*

Agents of Evangelisation ought to be proven christians, well versed in the Word of God and experienced witnesses in christian tradition, fulfilled in socio-economic life; men and women who love God; who have interest in godly and church affairs and are willing to make sacrifices, spend quality time and talents for Christ and his church. St. Paul appears as an ideal in this context. He was first and foremost a lawyer who studied under Gamaliel as well as a tent maker and thirdly the evangeliser of the Gentiles. He could then afford to be independent and not constitute a burden to anyone in his evangelising mission.

Where formal education is given to agents of evangelisation, such Institutes must strive to meet up with the standard set within a local context. Such Institutes must not only be locally and internationally recognised but must be able to compete with their counterparts and above all excel in quality and output.[157]

Authentic evangelisation can well be realised where the clergy and religious apply the principles of evangelisation in their life and ministry. The lay people, who are evangelisers ought to become as a matter of primary necessity self-fulfilled people in life, as St. Paul or as professional in one area of life or another, banker, business, politician, hand-worker, etc. and in these they bring Christ into it, such that any one dealing with such a person would at the end exclaim, *this man indeed, has been with the Lord*

*Jesus*. This is considered basic and has other numerous important implications and consequences.

## Goals of Evangelisation

The first goal of evangelisation is to evangelise the faithful. Each and every christian is throughout his or her life called to a deeper and deeper conversion to the gospel. One may be able to point to a date on which one was converted for the first time. But there is no date on which that conversion is concluded short of death. If our conversion is not on-going, we are in effect spiritually dead.

Who are the first people to whom we are sent to bring the Gospel? The correct answer is to our fellow Catholics. And each catholic here is both evangeliser and evangelised. This is not a task for the ministers alone. Who evangelises the clergy? The members of the laity do. As the clergy share their faith stories with the laity, have they not very often experienced a deeper dimension of the gospel hearing it from another person's perspective and history?

Naturally the minister has a more structured role within the church and within the evangelisation ministry. It is the minister's job to keep the vision alive for the community. And this happens primarily through preaching.

Some communities have set aside one Sunday in a month to focus on evangelisation. While this may be one way to begin, it also misses the point. Evangelisation is not something special we do. It is a crucial part of who we are. While it may be beneficial to heighten consciousness about evangelisation with a special homily each month, the ideal would be to allow the evangelising vision to permeate every homily. Not every homily would be about evangelisation, but the perspective would inform each homily.

At present one still struggles to come to full grip with the whole vocabulary of Evangelisation. The word elicits from many Catholics visions of going from door to door, asking whether you are saved. Most Catholics feel uncomfortable with such tactics. And rightly too, for there is a catholic style and flavour to Evangelisation. But it will take time for Catholics to learn and practice this new way.

It will take time for this vision to permeate our faith. There is no quick fix. So proceed slowly. Test things. Evaluate things and situations. Share ideas within the parish and with other communities. Slowly you will come to see the faith through the eyes of evangelisation. It will become a crucial dimension of who the Catholics are. Gone will be the day when people will think that you have to be born a catholic in order to really be catholic. We will be changed, and so will people and even cultures.

For although the first goal of evangelisation is to fellow Catholics and their communities, there are two other goals as well. Good news has been entrusted to the Church, how does it reach out in welcome to those who do not have faith? There seems to be more non-believers in this world we live than people who believe.

By people of faith, one does not limit oneself to Catholics or even to christians, but include those who embrace other religions as well. Most of the people or neighbours do not have a spiritual vision by which they understand and live their lives. The church has a great treasure. The church must seek therefore ways and means to share that treasure with others.

She searches for ways to enable people of no faith to hear the good news of Jesus. The gospel is not unchanging. Yes, Jesus Christ is the same yesterday, today, and tomorrow. But the actual words, ideas, and media it employs to communicate this gospel must change with the times and the culture. How does she tell her story of faith in such a way that a twenty first century Nigerian, African, world, can come to accept its truth? To do so, she has to speak in the context of modern science, psychology and communications.[158]

A next group consists of those who no longer actively practice the faith. Inactive Catholics form the second largest religious group in the world today. Sure, they have heard the gospel. But they have heard it in fragments of distorted manner, so that it did not bring them life. They may have been wounded by the church. Perhaps they simply drifted away and are just waiting for a simple invitation to come home. Whatever the reason, the church through her members, needs to go in search of them so that they too might hear again or for the first time the freeing power of the gospel. It is up to the church to take the initiative to welcome them back into their family of faith. Does the church really care that these relapsed members are not with her. How can she genuinely manifest her concern for these people outside authentic Evangelisation?

With other christians, the church share a common faith. In dialogue with them, she grows with them through a deeper encounter with Jesus Christ. With other religions, she deepens with them through sharing experiences such as praying together a common understanding of God.

Catholics are greatly indebted to the scripture scholarship developed by protestants in the last century. Many Catholics have rediscovered their own contemplative tradition by learning to meditate from Buddhists. And the church in turn may have helped to spur the new phenomenon of socially engaged Buddhism emerging out of Buddhism's encounter with the West. All of this is Evangelisation. It is not proselytising. The church is not out to convert the other, although that may happen. She shares her faith with one another while she continues on her own paths, her common pilgrimage toward God.[159]

The third goal of evangelisation is the local culture. How can the saving Word touch and transform the common life of the people in a given social context? Here one encounters enormous issues such as peace and justice, the sanctity of human life, the fate of the poor, and concern for the environment. What does the gospel say to these concerns? How can economics, politics and society be leavened by gospel compassion?

How can one contribute to the building up of good neighbourhood and community? How does one care for the poor and victims of injustice? How does one reach out to the wounded? How does one address issues of violence and abuse in one's own community? All these people and situations need to hear the good news. The social action ministries have to proclaim the good news in ways that touch and transform a local culture. As one allows the evangelising vision to shape one's own appreciation of the gospel message, one will come to see that to reach out to others with kindness and hope as the church has been reached out to, is essential to following Jesus.[160]

It will take many rigorous forms of formation for one to begin thinking with an evangelising mindset. How can one for instance think of

Liturgy as evangelisation? How does one make the liturgy more inviting and emphasise the sending forth? Do the songs and music one chooses promote the church's mission? Does one look at the roles of the various liturgical ministers as being evangelistic? For example, are there greeters each Sunday to welcome people? Is someone in charge of a programme for welcoming new-comers? The main objectives of Evangelisation is to give birth to new christians who see themselves as signs of good news to others.

## Evangelisation: Some Biblical Background

Evangelisation finds a most favourable background in the biblical mandate of Christ to his disciples where he says: *All authority in heaven and on earth has been given to me. Go therefore and make disciples of all nations, baptising them in the name of the Father and of the Son and of the Holy Spirit, teaching them to observe all that I have commanded you;.... Matt. 28:18-20.*

The effect of this brief pericope on the life of the christian church has been incalculable. No part of the Bible (with the possible exception of the letter to the Romans) has done more to give christians the vision of a world-wide church. It has sent them to all nations, bearing the message of salvation through Christ, with which are linked the responsibility and privilege of obeying his words.[161] This text tells of a final commission from the risen Lord to his disciples. The disciples are to **baptise, make disciples** and **teach**. According to other evangelists the disciples are to be witnesses and to preach repentance.[162] That is what Christianity is all about. For John the Evangelist, Christianity is a church whose membership must be holy, reconciling, and filled with love for the brotherhood [163] (cf. Jn. 20:23). Thus the commission is regarded as an empowerment with the Holy Spirit to forgive sins and to bring all to Christ. All put together, the mandate is to baptise, make disciples, teach, witness, and a call to be holy.

The evangelist ends his Gospel with a claim *All Authority;* a great commission with *all nations* of the world as its *scope; baptising* and *teaching* being the components of the *main task;* and with its *End* and *Aim* and with a great statement of fact not just a promise – *always.*

# All Authority

Authority in this sense means supreme right to appoint to office. It means right to require obedience because of love poured out unto death, and now triumphant in the eternal kingdom. It means governance in both earth and heaven. A true faith is not chosen by human beings: it chooses them. It is not a garment that we can *don or doff,* but the very life, which Christ claims to be the Lord of. It really requires someone with power[164] and authority[165] to command. What does one do with this command? To allow it to fall on deaf ears? Or to deny the authority of Christ? Not seldom his commands run counter to what seems to us to be practical wisdom. He has right to command. The command is spoken in the gentleness of love and the rigour of holiness. He shares with all the hazards of obedience. The issue of his dictates is joy. But authority is his, in heaven and on earth.

Obviously, the command is to be fulfilled with the best of one's ability and in most loving obedience as he clearly demonstrated in his incarnation[166] (Jn. 1: 14: *...and the Word took flesh and dwelt among us;* Phil. 2:6-12: *Jesus did not count his equality with God a thing to be grasped, he emptied himself...*). He was not under any compulsion or what is today referred to as compelled obedience which is characteristic of dictators or such rulers who have only their authority to invoke and to fall back on. Good leaders like God, do not compel their subjects, or threaten them or brandish their powers and authorities but by a loving expression or exercise of power and authority that ultimately elicit loving and filial obedience as was clearly evident in Christ. As Christ was most obedient to the Father, so also should the Church in her members be excellent witnesses to Christ as they carry the Good-news to all the ends of the earth.

# All Nations – The Scope of Evangelisation

This has been a recurrent theme in the teaching of Christ. Early christians in mission countries for instance learnt of Christ through christian missionaries, and they ought in thanksgiving to share the gift they have received. Joy constrains them. Joy must be shared. For joy shared is joy doubled and sorrow shared is sorrow halved. A doctor would be called recreant if he did not proclaim his discovery of cure, and the Christian is a recreant if he fails to tell the inexhaustible peace and power of Christ. A christian must be like the hen that shouts on meeting a fortune: *Okuku na etili uha nkpu*. But even when one does not feel either gratitude or joy, even when one's mood is low, one is still under orders: *go therefore*....

Authority is Christ's but he stoops to use the human hand and heart to work his will.... Even when his followers have not always obeyed (Acts 11:1-18), the marching order remains: *go therefore*....

## Components of the Main Task

These include *make disciples* of all nations, *baptise* them and *teach* them ...

When the words were first spoken, they were a dozen men, none of whom seemed worth mentioning in a history book, and even the Leader was taken to be the illusion of an impassioned woman. Yet it was said to be the wildest of dreams to believe that people of many lands could have one mind in religion as seen best in Christianity. They must have one mind or die in their violent hates. The logic of history points to the alternative -- Christ or chaos.[167]

It will be recalled here that the covenant was made with the Jews. The will of Christ in this command means that the covenant of peculiarity made with the Jews should now be extended to include the non-Jews. When the apostles were first sent out, they were forbidden to go into the way of the Gentiles, but on the strength of this commission, they were sent to all nations. Secondly, the salvation wrought by Christ should be offered to all without exception. No one should be excluded as long as one does not by one's unbelief and impenitence exclude oneself. For the apostles and the Church today, they should preach a common salvation.[168]

The commission to all nations means in effect that Christianity should leaven all facets of human life and society. It should influence in all its entirety the national constitutions of the world in such a way that the kingdoms of the world should become Christ's kingdom and their kings the church's nursing-fathers. Christ in other words enjoins the church through her members then and now, to leave no stones unturned, to expend every ounce of their energy, to employ every fibre in their being, to unreservedly put the best in them to make the nations of the world christian nations.

Christ the Mediator has set up a kingdom in the world through his Paschal Mystery. He expects the church to bring the nations to be his scholars; raising an army, enlist the nations of the earth under his banner. The work the apostles had to do was to set up the christian religion in all places, and it was an honourable work. The achievements of the mighty heroes of the world were nothing compared to this task. The heroes conquered the nations for themselves, and made them miserable. The apostles and the present church ought to conquer the nations for Christ and make them happy.[169]

As the church goes to all nations, she must preach the Good-news, work miracles among them, and persuade them to come in themselves and bring their children with them into the Church of Christ and admit them into the church of Christ by washing them with water. The baptism must be administered in the name of the Father and of the Son and of the Holy Spirit. The people are admitted into the church by the authority from heaven and not from man or earth. The ministers act not on their own authority, but by the authority of the three Persons in the Godhead. They call on the name of the (*eis to onoma*) Father, Son and Holy Spirit which is the summary of the first principles of the christian religion.[170]

Being baptised, the church professes solemnly her assent to the Scripture-Revelation concerning God, the Father, Son and Holy Spirit. She professes solemnly her consent to a covenant relation with God the Father, Son and Holy Spirit. Baptism thus is a sacrament, that is, it is an oath. It is an oath of renunciation or abjuration by which one renounces the world and the flesh as rivals with God for the throne in the human hearts. It is an oath of allegiance, by which one resigns and gives up oneself to God, to be his *body*, *soul* and *spirit*; to be governed by his will and made happy in his favour. One becomes his people so that the form of homage flows ordinarily.[171]

It is into the name of the Father that one is baptised. In effect believing him to be the Father of the Lord Jesus Christ and the Father of all christians, especially as the Creator, Preserver and Benefactor to whom therefore one resigns oneself, to be the ruler, as free agent by his law and as the chief good and the highest end. It is into the name of the Son, the Lord Jesus Christ, the Son of God, that one is baptised. In baptism, one assents as Peter did, *thou art Christ, the Son of the living God.*[172] In baptism one consents as Thomas did, *my Lord and my God.*[173] In baptism one takes Christ to be one's Prophet, Priest and King, and gives up oneself to be taught, saved and ruled by him. It is into the name of the Holy Spirit that one is baptised. One gives oneself up to the conduct and unction and operations of the Holy Spirit. The Spirit thus becomes one's sanctifier, teacher, guide and comforter.[174]

Those that are thus baptised and enrolled among the disciples of Christ must be taught.[175] They must be taught to observe all things, *whatsoever I have commanded you.* Christianity is not like a buffet party, where one can pick and choose. It is rather a matter of take it all or leave it all. All the baptised, therefore, must submit to the teaching of those whom he sends. He enlists soldiers that he may train them up for his service. All the baptised are thereby obliged to make the command of Christ their rule of life. One is by baptism bound and must obey. They are to observe what Christ has commanded. Due obedience to the commands of Christ, requires a diligent observation.

They are to observe all things that he has commanded without exception. That includes all the moral duties and all the instituted ordinances. They are to confine themselves to the commands of Christ, and not to diminish from them, and not to add to them. They are to learn their duty according to the law of Christ, from those whom he has appointed to be teachers in his school. The duty of the apostles of Christ and his ministers is to teach the commands of Christ. They must teach them, and in the knowledge of them christians must be trained up. The heirs of heaven must be under tutors and governors until they come to age. This is the assurance he gives them of his spiritual presence with them in the execution of this commission. Baptism could rightly be described as a sacrament of belongingness, incorporation, participation and membership into the christian fold.

## I am with you always even to the end of the world

Christ was now about to leave the apostles. His bodily presence was now to be removed from them, and this grieved them. But he assures them of his spiritual presence. *I am with you.* In effect, my Spirit is with you, the Comforter shall abide with you.[176] I am with you and not against you. I am with you to take your part and be on your side. I am with you and not absent from you, not at a distance, but I am a very present help.

So Christ was now sending them to set up his kingdom in the world. And then does he reasonably promise them his presence with them in order to carry them on through the difficulties they were likely to meet. I am with you to bear you up, to plead your cause with you in all your services and in all your sufferings. I am with you to make your ministry most effectual for the discipline of the nations. It was an unlikely thing that they should persuade people to become the disciples of a crucified Jesus.

## Always Even to the End of the World.

Christians shall have his constant presence; *always* – *pasas tas emeras* – everyday. In effect, I will be with you on Sabbath days and week days; fair days and fowl days; winter days and summer days. Since his resurrection, he had appeared to them now and then. But he assures them now and then, he assures them that they would have his spiritual presence without interruption. The God of Israel the Saviour is sometimes a God that hides himself [177] but never a God that absents himself; sometimes in the dark, but never at a distance.

They shall have his perpetual presence, even to the end of the world. This is hastening towards its period. And even till then the christian religion shall, in one part of the world or other, be kept up, and the presence of Christ continued with his ministers. I am with you to the end of the world. I am with you and your writings. There is a divine power going along with the scriptures of the New Testament, not only preserving them in being, but producing strange effects by them, which will continue to the end of time. I am with you and your successors. I am with all who thus baptise and thus teach. This is an encouraging word to all the faithful ministers of Christ, that what was said to the apostles was said to them all, I will never leave you , nor forsake you.

Christ bade his church a farewell which is very remarkable. I am with you always.... I leave you and yet still with you. In the book of Revelation, he bids another farewell (22:20). By this it is clear that he did not part in anger, but in love, and that it is his will that the church should keep up both her communion with him and her expectation of him.

One final word draws one's attention – *Amen*. The word is not a cipher intended only for a concluding word like *finis* at the end of a book. It rather describes Christ's confirmation of this statement of fact. *Lo, I am with you always.* It is instead his *Amen*, in whom all the promises are. It describes the church's concurrence with it, in their desire, prayer and expectation. It is the evangelist's *Amen – so be it*, blessed Lord. The church's *Amen* to Christ's promises turns them into prayers.

How then does one make disciples of all nations, how does one baptise and teach? What methods are available. What happened to the old methods. There is absolute need to review the earlier methods. The method must be reviewed and apostolic zeal renewed. One must today apply the new approach in evangelisation, namely, new in zeal, new in method and new in expression. If other lands refuse Christ at our hands, the fault is not in Christ, but in the unsuitability of our hands; and the solving of the problem is not in our silence, but in our penitence and thorough examination of conscience.

## Conclusion

One needs to examine and heed the recent call of the Holy Father as contained in Lk. 5:4: *put out into deep water and pay out your net for a catch – Duc in altum!* Luke tells this great story of the miraculous draught of fishes which points ultimately to the calling of the disciples as one of the many signs which Jesus did, which had not been written in the foregoing books.

First, the people pressed upon him to hear the word of God. They flocked about him! They showed respect to his preaching. The people relished good preaching, they pressed to hear the word of God, they coveted to hear it. Second, *imagine the poor conveniences Christ had for preach-*

*ing:* he stood by the lake of Gennesaret, upon a level with the crowd, so that they could neither see him nor hear him; he was lost among them, he was crowded, and in danger of being crowded into the water. What must he do? there were two ships, or fishing boats brought to shore, one belonging to Simon and Andrew the other to Zebedee and his sons. Christ entered into that ship that belonged to Simon, and begged of him that he would lend it to him for a pulpit. Therein he sat down and taught the people the good knowledge of the Lord.

Third, when Christ had finished his preaching, he ordered Peter to apply himself to the business of his calling again: *launch out into the deep and let down your nets.* It was not the Sabbath day, and therefore, as soon as the preaching was over, he set them to work. One could rightly ask, with what cheerfulness may one go about the duties of one's calling when one has been in the mount with God? It is one's wisdom and duty to manage one's religious exercises in such a manner that they may befriend the worldly business. Therefore, to manage the worldly business in such a way that it may be no enemy to one's religious exercises.

Furthermore, Peter having attended to Christ in his preaching, Christ will accompany him in his fishing. He stayed with Christ at the shore, and now Christ will launch out with him into the deep. Christ then ordered Peter and his ship's crew to cast their nets into the sea, which they did in obedience to him, though they had been hard at it all night and had caught nothing.

It may be good to observe here how melancholic their business had now been, Master, we have toiled all the night and have taken nothing. One would have thought that this should have excused them from hearing the sermon; but it was more refreshing and reviving to them than the softest slumbers. But they mentioned it to Christ, when he bids them go a fishing again.

Some callings are more toilsome than others, and more perilous; yet Providence has so ordered it for the common good that there is no useful calling so discouraging but some others have a genius for it. Those who follow their business, and get abundance by it with a great deal of ease, should think with compassion about those who cannot follow theirs but with a great fatigue, and hardly get a bare livelihood by it. Be the calling ever so laborious, it is good to see people diligent in it.

These fishermen that were thus industrious Christ singled out for his favourites. Even those who are most diligent in their business often meet with disappointments; they toiled all night yet caught nothing. One must do one's duty and then leave the rest to God. When one is tied with one's worldly business, and crossed in one's worldly affairs, one is welcomed to come to Christ, and present one's case before him.

In spite of all, the apostles obeyed. Though they had toiled all night, yet if Christ bid them, they would renew their toil. For every fresh service they shall have a fresh supply of sufficient grace. Though they have got nothing, yet if Christ bid them let down for a draught, they will hope to get something. One must not abruptly quit the callings wherein one is called because one has not the success in them which one promised oneself. The ministers of the Gospel must continue to let down that net, though they have perhaps toiled long and caught nothing. This indeed is thank worthy, to continue unwearied in one's labours, though one sees not the success of them. One is indeed likely to speed well when one follows the guidance of Christ's word.

The draught of fish they caught was so much beyond what was ever known that it amounted to a miracle. The catch was so great that they needed more hands to draw it ashore.

By this great draught of fishes, Christ intended to show his dominion in the seas as well as on dry land, over its wealth and waves. He intended hereby to confirm the doctrine he had just now preached out of Peter's ship. One may suppose that the people on shore stayed halting about there, to see what he would do next; and this miracle immediately following would be a confirmation to their faith, of his being at least a teacher come from God. He intended hereby to repay Peter for the loan of his boat. Christ's recompenses for services done to his name are abundant. They are super abundant.

He intended hereby also to give a specimen to those who were to be his ambassadors to the world, of the success of their embassy, that though they might for a time, and in one particular place, toil and catch nothing, yet they should be instrumental to bringing in many to Christ, and enclose many in the gospel net.

Christ had to contend with poor conveniences for his preaching. The same applies today to all those who are engaged seriously in evangelisation. Christ solved the problem of poor convenience by asking Peter to lend him his boat for a pulpit. Peter did not hesitate to give up his boat, because the Lord needed it.

As Peter attended to the needs of Christ, Christ in turn attended to Peter in the fishing business. The generosity of Christ is in superabundance. Not only that your fishing boat will be filled, but in a double form and to a sinking point. Identify with Christ and his church and you will never regret it. Give Christ a challenge.

One is consoled by the Lord himself. No matter how melancholic the evangelisation may turn out to be, one must never give up. The collective faith and obedience of the fishermen earned them the draught of fishes. The faith each christian has, is a faith mission. Faith must be both individual and collective. In this lies the thrust of the new era of Evangelisation and its new strategy.

# CHAPTER SIX

# LITURGICAL GESTURES AND POSTURES

Postures and gestures play a great role in the meaningful celebration of the liturgy. As a disciplined religion, postures and gestures are not left to the whims and caprices of anyone to determine. The church has her determined postures and gestures as she celebrates her liturgy. These include standing, sitting, kneeling and others.

The significance which the church attaches to these postures is well articulated in the Revised General Instruction on the Roman Missal. It says among other things that the gestures and posture of the priest, deacon and the ministers, as well as the people, should allow the whole celebration to shine with dignity and noble simplicity, demonstrating the full and true meaning of each of their diverse parts, while fostering the participation of all.[178]

Therefore, greater attention needs to be paid to what is laid down by liturgical law and by the traditional practice of the Roman Rite, for the sake of the common spiritual good of the people of God, rather than to personal inclinations or arbitrary choice.[179] The uniformity in posture to be observed by all taking part is a sign of the unity of the members of the christian community gathered for the sacred liturgy. It both expresses and fosters the spiritual attitude of those assisting.[180]

Observations reveal that the church has given instructions with regard to when to stand, when to sit, when to kneel and when to move.[181] What about other gestures like striking the chest at the *confiteor*, the kiss of peace before communion, the issue of sticking out one's tongue at communion?

In the light of revisiting these issues, one is expected to re-examine the significance of these gestures against the cultural background of the people. What the universal church does with these gestures and postures is one, and whether they are universally accepted or conform with the cultural sentiments and the genius of the people or not is another. Do these gestures and postures as they are really express the same meaning to the various people that belong to the Roman rite? In other words is one not actually expected to enrich these gestures and postures with the proper meaning they have for the people even if it means changing them completely and replacing them with what makes meaning to the people? This is against the axiom that whatever is obnoxious in a culture should not be introduced into the liturgy. For instance there are cultures that frown at an adult being fed in the mouth in public or a man feeding a woman who is not his wife in public, like in some parts of Uganda and in some parts of Igboland, particularly in Ezeagu Local Government Area of Enugu State of Nigeria.

Within such a cultural context, the distribution of the holy communion in the mouth ought to give way to a better and acceptable gesture, perhaps passing the communion in the ciborium round for people to take and feed themselves. There is also the optional practice of putting it in the hand of the recipient who takes it with care and decorum and consumes. The following common gestures and postures need to be reviewed against an African background:

i.   Standing
ii.  Sitting
iii. Kneeling
iv.  Movement/Procession
v.   Striking the chest,
vi.  Liturgical Silence
vii. kiss of Peace

# i.  Standing

The recent instruction stipulates that the faithful should stand from the beginning of the opening song or when the priest enters until the end of the
opening prayer or collect. The assembly should stand for the singing of the
*Alleluia* before the Gospel reading and while the Gospel itself is being proclaimed. During the profession of faith and the general intercession they
stand. Next the assembly stands from the invitatory, *pray that our sacrifice....*

Without prejudice to the pre-eminent position given to the proclamation of the gospel which is done standing vis-à-vis other readings which are
done in sitting posture, one could correctly ask how does a local church
give pre-eminence by way of posture to the climax of the readings such as
the gospel. The importance of the gospel in the eucharistic celebration is
such that it is even heralded by a series of ceremonies. First, the singing of
the *alleluia* verse at the intonation all stand, the procession by the deacon
and in his absence the priest, the asking for blessing by the deacon and or a
priest before the bishop and when a priest is the celebrant, the deacon asks
for the blessing, the incensation that follows.

And then at the end, there is also the recessional protocol, kissing of
the book by the bishop if he is the principal celebrant and the blessing of
the people with the book of the gospel or kissing the book by the reader in
the absence of the bishop. An outstanding event during the proclamation of
the gospel is that all stand until it is over.

Standing generally in the liturgical celebration is a symbolic posture
of the resurrection. Christians are discouraged from kneeling down during
paschal tide, especially during the recitation of the Rejoice O Queen of
Heaven (*Regina caeli laetare...*), and to stand up immediately after the elevation of the chalice at Sunday Mass. Furthermore, the singing of the Litany of the Saints on Sundays of the year and during the Easter Octave is
done standing in order to underscore the same posture of victory of Christ
over death.

When a priest stands at the Altar or Ambo, there representing Christ
and His church, his posture should suggest confidence, based on the per-

manent gift God has imparted on him. At the same time, he should convey a humble sense of his role in ministering the Sacred Mysteries, human actions and signs which are divine. Because he sets the examples for others, he should expect the same standard of decorum from all who assist in the sanctuary.[182] Given all that with regard to the theological significance of standing posture, it would still be necessary to revisit the posture in the light of cultural values particularly during the gospel reading.

In some parts of Igboland, standing position would not normally be associated with receiving an important message from a god or an important personality, the *Igwe* for instance. People usually sit. The same applies to serious discussions. Sitting position on such occasions as these has the psychology of being accorded dignity and deeper appreciation. On receiving the message in sitting position, the nerves are relaxed, the faculties are attentive, and the intellect is receptive. These pave the way for more receptivity, better listening, mature deliberation, thoughtfulness, composure, meditation and internalisation of what is being delivered. An Igbo proverb has it that ***whoever stands at such occasions is prone to scolding and unfriendly utterances*** – *onye kwu oto aghaghi ikwu ajo okwu;* secondly, *okwu oto aghaghi ikwuta abia/obia*: ***one who stands often begets an unwelcome visitor.*** Such connotations as these often go with standing in a public gathering and, therefore, may not enhance active participation in the liturgy.

In a typical African traditional worship, serious messages, especially from the oracles of the gods, are listened to in a sitting position. Only casual pieces of information are usually received while standing. For instance, sending a child or an inferior on an errand by a superior, the inferior or the child receives the message standing while being pre-occupied with hearing the last word for him to rush out and deliver the message uninvolved as the case may be.

Even to receive a special guest in the council of *ozo* titled men or the *Igwe's* cabinet, the hosts are usually seated while the guest with hat removed goes round to shake hands, until finally he is also seated for the meeting. Against an *Igbo* cultural pattern of life, the proclamation of the gospel could well be received if the posture tallies with the people's way of life.

## ii.    Sitting

The liturgical significance which the RGIRM accords sitting postures tallies largely with the African understanding of sitting down in worship. According to the document under review, the assembly sits during the readings, the responsorial psalm, the homily, the preparation of gifts, and during meditation after the reception of Holy Communion.[183] These are very important moments in the celebration of the Eucharist. It goes even to buttress the earlier argument that has been presented in favour of sitting during the proclamation of the gospel.

## iii.    Kneeling

Kneeling belongs rightly to the catholic tradition of worship. It is one of the distinctive features found in the catholic church which is absent in the protestant and Pentecostal churches. One hardly finds kneelers in these other churches. Kneeling in the catholic traditional worship is based on the action of Christ: then he withdrew from them, about a stone's throw away, and knelt down and prayed (Lk. 22:41). In Acts of the Apostles, it is said that Peter sent everyone out of the room and knelt down and prayed (9:40).[184]

RGIRM stipulates that the assembly should kneel during consecration, except when prevented by reason of health, lack of space, the number of people present, or some other good reason. [185] The good reason is unspecified. Perhaps one should consider lack of proper provision for kneeling, for example, in an unfinished church building, makeshift structure, open air celebrations.

The document further states that those who do not kneel at the consecration ought to make a profound bow when the priest genuflects after the consecration. The challenge comes then with the demand that the Conference of Bishops could decide otherwise regarding the universal gestures as contained in the document as follows: it is up to the Conference of Bishops to adapt the gestures and postures in the Order of the Mass to the custom and reasonable traditions of the people according to the norm of law.[186]

The Conference, however, must make sure that such adaptations correspond to the meaning and character of each part of the celebration. Where it is the custom that the people remain kneeling from the end of the Sanctus until the end of the Eucharistic Prayer, this is laudably retained.[187]

Furthermore, for the sake of observing a uniformity in gestures and postures during the same celebration, the faithful should obey the directions which the deacon or lay person or the priest give during the celebration, according to whatever is indicated in the liturgical books.[188]

Kneeling in christian liturgy designates humility and adoration. In some circumstances it may symbolise supplication and contrition. When one thinks of kneeling as a liturgical posture, it tends to exclude some people in the African set up. In Igboland, an adult hardly kneels down for what the posture stands for. Ordinarily in Igbo culture, to ask an adult to kneel down in public is not a *modus vivendi*. To do so would be the height of humiliation for such a man. Humiliation in this sense should not be confused with humility, being a virtue that tends to be lost in the act of humiliation. Considering kneeling as a part of body language in worship, what is obnoxious in the culture should stay clear in the worshipping form of the church.

Two important consequences arise from this consideration. How best can an African express reverential adoration at consecration? Second, how best can an African express humility or contrition apart from kneeling? For the former one could consider standing up with a slight bow as one would do on greeting a superior or in some places even prostration by all as a sign of complete submission, adoration, reverence and worship. For the latter, a suitable posture is sitting down on a low stool with head bent downwards and supported by the palm of the hand. Alternatively there is sitting down with hands folded and pressed on the chest. To see an African in such a posture leaves no one in doubt regarding the mood of the person.

## iv. Movement – Procession

A sound sense of liturgical ceremony starts with the way each person moves in procession to the sanctuary. All who are involved in the liturgical celebration, minor ministers, lectors, deacons and the celebrant, ought to move with dignity, decorum, without haste, yet without seeming to be ponderous or pompous.

The joyous mood of the celebration has to be reflected in the way the movement of the ministers is being carried out. It does not have to depict a sorrowful mood, for the liturgy is the celebration of the mysteries of Christ which ends up in joyful expectation and hope. Movement in the liturgical celebration does not need to degenerate into mere mechanical walk without a purpose or meaning. It goes beyond an ordinary match past. It is something other than the match of an angry mob or a demonstration. Movement or procession is considered to be a form of gesture. It takes place when for instance, the priest with the deacon and minor ministers go to the Altar, when the lay readers proceed from their seats to the Altar and to the Ambo for the readings of the Mass, when the deacon carries the *Evangelia* or the Book of the Gospels to the ambo before the proclamation of the Gospel, when the faithful present the gifts or come forward to receive Communion, and finally when the celebration is over with the recession into the sacristy.[189]

RGIRM recommends that such movements, especially by the priests, deacons and laity at the moments of procession for the offertory and communion and recession should be carried out becomingly in keeping with the norms prescribed for each while the liturgical songs proper to them are being sung.[190] A review of this recommendation within African culture especially during the offertory evokes certain reactions.

Given the natural exuberance of the Africans in worship, movement to the Altar at the offertory betrays the joyous sentiments of the Africans, especially Nigerians, particularly *Ndigbo*. Incidentally here is one area where inculturation shines out in a very eloquent manner. One sees here a deep sentiment of reverence as people carry their gifts of cash and kind to the Altar during the offertory. After the normal bringing on of bread, wine and water, people match to the Altar dancing to the rhythm of the local music.

It therefore ought to be recommended that liturgical movements be conducted in the best possible manner which a local church deems fit as long as they do not constitute distractions. Such movements or procession should instead enhance the active, conscious and plenary participation of the assembly in the celebration.

## v.  Striking the Chest at Confiteor

The Roman rite prescribes striking the chest three times at the moment of saying, *through my fault,* during the confession of sins. The body language of striking the chest at this point in the liturgical celebration does not seem to express truly and fully the sorrowful sentiment of an Igbo Christian. The gesture has a contrary meaning associated with striking the chest. Instead of contrition which it has in the Roman liturgy, among *Ndigbo* it means defiance or a threat. From the point of view of defiance, an Igbo strikes the chest hard to underscore the fact that, *I did it with a bit of corresponding nodding of the head, after all what can you do to me.* From the point of view of threat, it sounds like, *you did this to me and striking the chest, wait until I come out and you will see.* On account of long practice of striking the chest, the gesture has become generally accepted rather than being an authentic African way of expression of sorrow and repentance. The gesture hitherto has become more of a convention rather than a conviction. Convention must give way to conviction, especially in matters of religion and worship.

Surely, for *Ndigbo*, true contrition is best expressed by placing the two arms in an x-form on the chest. This gesture underscores sorrow. Alternatively is to place the back of the right palm on top of the palm of the left, alternating the gesture as often as one recites the most pleading part of the prayer: *through my fault, through my fault, through my most grievous fault....* In some parts of Ghana, this gesture is common, thus expressing the genuine contrition of the sinner before God and one another.

## vi.  Liturgical Silence

Silence forms an integral part of liturgical celebration. It requires to be duly qualified. Observance of silence in the liturgy fortifies one's attitude and disposition to pray better. The art of maintaining liturgical silence facilitates the continuity of the Church's ancient tradition. Silence conditions one to pray better. It brings about a conducive atmosphere for concentration, active, conscious and plenary participation. Absence of silence in the liturgy can easily give way to a mere talkative liturgy which edifies no one.

118

When the liturgy is celebrated with full ceremonial, good music, and devotion with time for silence, then the worshipping community can experience continuity with the living tradition of Western Catholic worship as it has developed over the centuries.[191]

Prayerful silence should be observed at the designated times as part of the celebration.[192] Its function depends on the time it occurs in each part of the celebration. Thus, at the penitential rite and again after the invitation to pray, all recollect themselves. Prayerful silence is observed at the conclusion of a reading and after the homily. It helps one to digest, internalise and personalise the message given at the homily. All meditate briefly on what has been heard; after communion, all praise God in silent prayer.[193]

Even before the celebration itself, it is praise-worthy for silence to be observed in the Church, in the sacristy and adjacent areas, so that all may dispose themselves for the sacred rites which are to be enacted in a devout and fitting manner.[194]

## Silence before Eucharistic Celebration

The Church should be open well before the liturgy for those who wish to pray privately. Silence is the best preparation for the celebration of the liturgy. Apart from suitable music, no intrusion on the people's right to tranquillity before the Eucharist should be tolerated, for example, musical or choral rehearsals, announcements which could be given later, or distractions in the sanctuary or elsewhere. People may meet and talk before Mass, but in an area set well apart from the place where the liturgy is about to be celebrated.[195]

## vii.   Kiss of Peace

Kiss of peace or Rite of peace takes place shortly before the reception of Holy Communion. By this rite the Church asks for peace and unity for herself and for the whole human family, and the faithful offer some sign of their ecclesial communion and mutual love for each other before receiving the Sacrament.[196]

The form for the giving of the sign of peace is left to the Conference of Bishops to determine in accord with the culture and customs of the people. Nevertheless, it is suitable that each person offer the sign of peace only to those nearby and in a dignified manner.[197]

Here one thinks quite naturally of the words of Christ: if you present your offering at the Altar and there you remember hat your brother has something against you, leave your offering at the Altar ad go first to reconcile yourself with your brother (cf. Matt. 5: 23-24). It is in this spirit that the new Zairian Rite placed the rite of peace before the bringing of the gifts for the eucharistic liturgy.[198]

The sign of peace is exchanged *pro opportunitate,* according to when it is judged opportune. It can be considered always opportune to signify communion in peace and mutual love. As for the sign itself, it is determined by the conference of Bishops according to the mentality and customs of different people.[199]

The gesture calls for radical review. First when best can this rite be celebrated taking cognisance of the significance such a gesture bears for a particular people? In addition to the above significance, for *Ndigbo*, the Kiss of peace should be located at three points in a celebration, without prejudice to the law that abhors repetition in liturgy. Just as there are several points in the celebration where *the Lord be with you* is said, because of the significance it has at each point, so also the kiss of peace should not be restricted only shortly before communion. Against the Igbo cultural background, the kiss of peace should take place at three different moments within the eucharistic celebration.

## Kiss of Peace at the Beginning of Celebration

Usually when people gather for a formal get-together, they shake hands with one another, to recognise who is who in the gathering. When people welcome each other at a celebration the danger of anonymity is ruled out. The timely greeting no doubt paves the way for a better active, conscious and plenary participation in the liturgy that is being celebrated.

## Kiss of Peace Before Communion

In addition to the reasons given above for the rite of peace, it brings about a collective reconciliation of the assembly before they commune with the Lord in the Eucharist. The ritual cleansing and fraternal reconciliation are very necessary for the worthy reception of the Lord in the holy communion.

## Kiss of Peace At Dismissal

As the assembly is dismissed with a liturgical mandate, (*Ite Missa est*), go the Mass is ended, it is recommended that the people shake hands with one another as a sign of solidarity in the missionary mandate which they have been given. Usually, after a formal gathering, people shake hands to bid each other farewell. The same could well apply to a liturgical assembly with corresponding expressions like God bless you and have a nice new week. Fraternal greeting like this gives the celebration both divine and human face, and saves it from mere arid and mechanical celebration.

## Modality of Celebrating Kiss of Peace in the African Context

The basic question here is how best the Kiss of peace can be celebrated given the fact that hand-shaking in some cultures has certain limitations. Put in another form, one must ask some basic questions bothering on the understanding people have about who gives the other handshake. In effect, within some cultural localities in Western Nigeria, it is unacceptable for an inferior to stick out his or her hand to shake a superior. Instead the inferior prostrates fully on the ground. One needs to find out within the culture what is obtainable. For instance:

    i.    how does a man greet a man in public? perhaps by a warm hand shake.

    ii.    How does a woman greet another woman in public?

    iii.    how does a man greet a woman who is not his wife in public and vice versa?

    iv.    How does a young man greet a fellow young man.

v. How does a young man greet a young lady who is not his sister in public and vice versa?

vi. How does a man greet a girl who is not his daughter?

vii. How does a woman greet a boy who is not his son?

Liturgical inculturation thus demands that these issues be correctly handled so that what the Church does would not be seen as atrocious or obnoxious.

## Conclusion

A sound sense of ceremonial is distinguished by meaningful gestures and postures that are involved. The rule is that whatever movement, gesture and posture one takes, it should lead to an enhanced active participation. They should never be considered as source of distraction by any stretch of imagination.

Every gesture or posture must be seen from its biblical, christian, cultural and pastoral perspectives before admitting such into the liturgy. For the sake of emphasis, whatever is not acceptable to the culture should not be introduced into the liturgy of the Church.

In matters affecting gestures and postures there should be mutual openness between culture and church. The two ought to enrich each other in the true spirit of liturgical inculturation.

# CHAPTER SEVEN

# LITURGICAL HOMILY

## Introduction

Liturgical homily can best be understood as an enriched lively commentary on the Word of God. The church has always venerated the divine Scriptures just as she venerates the Body of the Lord, since from the table of both the Word of God and Body of Christ she unceasingly receives and offers to the faithful the bread of life.[200] It has become the good wish of the Council Fathers of the Second Vatican that easy access to sacred Scripture should be provided for all the christian faithful[201] not only by merely reading the words of the sacred Scriptures but above all through exposure to biblically based homily.

The ground for the renewed vigour towards the abundant use of the Scriptures in the life of christians was softened especially by Pope Leo X111 in his encyclical letter, *Providentissimus Deus* (1833), by Pope Benedict XV in his letter *Spiritus Paraclitus* (1920), and by Pope Pius X11's *Divino Afflante Spiritu* (1943). Indeed, Sacred Scriptures are of paramount importance in the celebration of the liturgy especially in the eucharistic celebration.[202] For, it inspires the other prayers and songs of the eucharistic celebration, all the actions and signs of the liturgy derive their meaning from Scriptures.[203]

Against the background of the renewed importance of the Scriptures in the liturgy by the Fathers of the Second Vatican Council in relation to what obtains in the local churches, especially in some regions of the Nigerian Church, one cannot but begin to wonder how faithful the homilists have dutifully carried out this special assignment. The liturgy prefers the term homily to sermon because of the radical difference between the two.

There are innumerable preachers today, especially since the upsurge of charismatic movements and renewals, many christian sects and evangelism, gospel preachers and healers, but there are very few homilists.

Many of those who are meant to be preaching homilies seem to be carried away by the popular style of today's preaching hawkers. Characteristics of such popular preaching methods include singing and clapping *ad nauseam* and dancing all of which often consume the entire time allotted to preaching the homily. Sometimes these actions substitute for the homily, thus suggesting an unpreparedness of the homilist. Virtue lies in the middle (*Virtus in medio stat*) applies very much in the art of delivering homilies in the liturgical celebration, especially at the eucharistic celebration.

## Nature of Homily

Homily comes from the Greek word *homilia,* which means re-union, company, or familiar conversation. It shares in the very mystery of Christ.[204] By means of the homily, the mysteries of the faith and the guiding principles of the Christian life are expounded from the sacred texts during the course of the liturgical year. The homily is highly esteemed as part of the liturgy itself. Indeed, at those Masses which are celebrated on Sundays and holidays of obligation, with the people assisting, it should not be omitted except for a serious reason.[205]

The homily appears like familiar conversation, but it is at the same time the Word of God. It is similar to Jesus Christ who appeared like an ordinary man, but he was at the same time the Son of God. Granted that the homily does not possess the universal value possessed by the Sacred Scriptures from where the homily draws, it is God's word on the level of the celebrating community. The golden rule for the homilist is the following: If someone speaks, let it be as words of God (cf. 1 Pet. 4:11). For the listener, the golden rule is stated in what Paul said to the Thessalonians: You have welcomed the word not as a human word, but as what it really is, the Word of God (cf. 1 Thess. 2:13). Every homily should have this golden rule always in view.

Just as only the Spirit of God can transform the bread of the earth into the bread of heaven, thus only the grace of the Holy Spirit can transfigure familiar human words into true words of God. Hence, the principle of ancient exegesis formulated by Gregory the Wonder-Worker (+ circa 270) is valid for both the speaker and the listener: The same grace is needed for those who pronounce the prophecy (that is, the divine Word) as for those who hear it. And no one can understand the prophecy if the Spirit who prophesied does not grant him the understanding of his words.[206]

The homily is closely related to the Word of God that is proclaimed. It is of paramount importance towards sustaining the spiritual feeding of the faithful. It is part of the liturgy and cannot be done without as it contains the necessary source of nourishment for the Christian life. Ideally, it consists of the systematic exposition of the scriptural readings or of some particular aspect of them, or of some other texts taken from the Ordo or the Proper of the Mass for the day, having regard for the mystery being celebrated or the special needs of those who hear it.[207]

In preaching homilies, prominence should be given to the biblical texts among other texts, because, the sacred Scriptures above all the texts used in the liturgical assembly enjoy a special dignity. In the readings God speaks to his people, and Christ, present in his word, announces the good news of the gospel. By implication, it means that the liturgy of the Word ought to be celebrated with greatest possible reverence. Other readings from past or present, sacred or profane authors, may never be substituted for the word of God. The purpose of the homily is thus to explain the readings and make them relevant to the present audience.

With regard to the homily, which is closely related to the Word, the Fathers recommended that by means of the homily the mysteries of the faith and the guiding principles of the christian life are expounded from the sacred texts during the course of the liturgical year. The homily, therefore, is to be highly esteemed as part of the liturgy itself. In fact at those masses which are celebrated on Sundays and holidays of obligation, with the people assisting, it should not be omitted except for a serious reason. [208]

The Council considered the homily as of paramount importance for the sustained spiritual feeding of the faithful. According to the Council, the homily is part of the liturgy and is strongly recommended, for it is the necessary source of nourishment for the christian life. Ideally, its content should be an exposition of the scripture readings or of some particular aspect of them, or of some other texts taken from the Ordo or the Proper of the Mass for the day, having regard for the mystery being celebrated or the special needs of those who hear it.[209]

The Fathers went further to extol and exalt the prominence of the Bible by saying that: the sacred scripture, above all the texts used in the liturgical assembly, enjoys a special dignity. Therefore, the liturgy of the Word should be conducted with the greatest reverence. Other readings from past or present, sacred or profane authors, may never be substituted for the word of God.

The purpose of the homily is to explain the readings and make them relevant for present-day. The homily is the task of the priest; the faithful refrain from comments and dialogue. The liturgy of the word prepares for and leads into the liturgy of the Eucharist forming with it one act of worship. The two parts should not be celebrated separately at different times or in different places.[210] It must be well noted that with the Second Vatican Council, in its reforms on the liturgy, the role of the Bible has remarkably assumed a much higher role than it had in the pre- Second Vatican Council era. A lot of emphasis is now laid on the prominent role which the bible plays in the liturgical celebration. Second, formerly the biblical texts were read in Latin which very few people well understood, and of course the preaching of the homily was in English with the aid of an interpreter. But today, with the translation of the Bible into various languages and vernacular, the role of the Bible in the Liturgy has become more remarkable.

The importance of the homily in the liturgical celebration needs to be emphasised further. A very well proclaimed Word of God and well prepared homily nourish the faith of the members a great deal. It keeps the celebration alive. Such quality homilies are always appreciated. They are usually very challenging and never boring. The readings and the homilies are to be celebrated in the same manner as the words of consecration. They are as important as that. Just as the words of consecration cannot be uttered any how, the same applies to the readings and the homilies. The apostles in the early church refused to be distracted in order to have time for the Word and Prayer.[211]

The tendency today is to emphasise the celebration of the sacraments over and above the Word. This is the mentality which was inherited from the pre-Second Vatican Council period. Today more than ever, the opportunity has been given to get back to the Word, to read, to love and to preach the Word of God. Every homily must speak of the life, passion, death and resurrection of Christ, namely, the paschal mystery. This is the core or the kernel of every homily. Otherwise, the homily is something else. The Cross of Christ must not be found missing in homilies, especially against the background of a materialistic society that seems to be deviating from the Cross and going after a Cross-less Christ. The centrality of the paschal mystery of Christ must be sufficiently emphasised.

The homily is not first and foremost speaking about social problems but rather a commentary on the Word and the best commentary is from the bible itself, drawing instances from the Scriptures to corroborate the themes or the aspects of Christ's mystery that are being celebrated. That means that the ministers of the Word must make the bible their closest companion.

The Word of God, as it were, not only teaches, but convicts, heals and illumines. No wonder then what happens in some churches, after the celebration, the Word of God is enthroned on the Altar, and the Word then becomes really Emmanuel. The church has the tendency to lose many of her members as a result of this deficiency in handling the Word. This is because people come to the celebration and leave with spiritual malnutrition. They are rather over burdened with necro- or moribund liturgy.

But any where the Word of God is powerfully proclaimed and preached, (behind a powerful microphone or public address system), enriched with nourishing fruits of deep prayerful reflections, local idiomatic expressions, poetic forms, proverbs and wisdom tit-bits, with good liturgical and cultural music to help in digesting the Word and Signs, the situation is quite different. Such ceremonies are usually full and the christian life and culture boom. Then in response, the people take up responsibilities to solve social problems, because they are now fully armed with Christ, and all these of course lead to reverence to the Word of God and the sacrament being celebrated. There is absolute need to make extra effort now to proclaim the Word of God with dignity, and make the crucified Christ central in all things.

## At the Heart of the Homily lies the Paschal Mystery of Christ

At the heart of the homily is the paschal mystery of Christ. The image of the heart signifies the innermost core or centre of an organism, the starting point and terminus of the circulating blood. The heart is the vitalising centre without which life is impossible. As the principal organ, it supplies all areas of the body, even in their most minute parts, with the blood that is indispensable for life.[212]

The Paschal Mystery of Christ can be well understood in the broad and narrow senses. In the broad sense, it includes the incarnation, the birth, the public life, the ministry, the miracles, the doctrines, the passion, death, resurrection, ascension, Pentecost, sitting at the right hand of God, and the final coming of Christ in glory. That would mean the totality of what Christ is. Secondly, it has a very close connection with the entirety of the christian mystery which is summarised in the Church's creed: the Holy Trinity, Creation, Fall, Redemption, Sanctification, Grace, Mariology, Sanctorals, Sacraments, Death, Judgement, Heaven, Hell. It remains the central and focal point of all that the church believes and celebrates. The strict sense of the term includes simply the passion, death and resurrection of Christ.

The importance of the paschal mystery of Christ to the preaching of the homily cannot be over-emphasised. Actually, it is the nucleus, or better said, the vital axis of any homily that merits the name. It should be the nerve centre of all the preaching and all the catechesis derived from the life of worship, and should orient everything toward itself, for it is the central event in the history of redemption.[213]

## Critical Criteria For Assessment of Homilies

A homily should be:
1.   Coherent and well organised.
2.   Rooted in sound doctrine
3.   Characterised by precision
4.   Never embarrass with abuses or insinuations
5.   Display of sufficient mastery of the theme or topic
6.   Devoid of trivialities
7.   have concrete and vivid illustrations
8.   offer guiding principle/s to good Christian living
9.   Tailored to meet the needs of an audience
10.  have a tinge of newness to familiar topics

11. Lively and inspiring
12. Address current human life experiences
13. Utilise concrete circumstances of current living
14. Delivered with polished language, liturgy abhors vulgar or foul language
15. Message logically sequenced
16. Ability to stimulate behaviour modification
17. The preacher must be a model of what he preaches
18. Provide accompanying action for behaviour modification
19. Reasonably short, 15-20 minutes on Sunday, 5-8 minutes on weekdays, never too lengthy, and preferably written down, by this one could say a lot in a small space of time.
20. Well adapted to the group both linguistically and intellectually
21. In tune with the liturgical season or occasion
22. Spiritual lessons made permanently memorable through appropriate stories
23. Use relevant penetrating and thought provoking humour, make them laugh but make them think
24. Illustrate with edifying incidents and interesting anecdotes
25. Make effective use of Public Address System
26. Devoid of expensive dry jokes
27. Not nauseate with repetitions, flat jokes and hymns
28. With intermittent jokes and hymns reasonably timed and not over dramatised
29. Courageous in exposing the ills of the time
30. Hand down the eternal truth of the Gospel without fear or favour
31. A captivating introduction
32. Be based on the Paschal Mystery of Christ
33. Be a unit and synthesis of the three Sunday readings into a coherent message or two daily readings of the weekday
34. Well concluded with the major highlights
35. Preach this homily to yourself before the Blessed Sacrament only after then can you go out to preach it to others.[214]

# Conclusion

Homily is an integral part of the liturgical celebration. It is quite different from sermon. A homily can draw from the biblical texts, readings, responsorial psalms, alleluia verse, the liturgical season and the euchological formulary of the celebration. A sound homily has the tremendous effect of building up the spiritual fortification of the members of the church. The members feel satisfactorily nourished by a well prepared and masterly delivered homily. With its soothing traits, the church is able to withstand all her trials and tribulations. With its challenging tendency, the church braces for action in the continuous christian warfare and ultimately leading to the perfect praise of God in their lives.

It is a liturgical act. It is characterised by exposition of the text with little background, exhortation and challenges, and must have bearing with realities of the life of the audience. Its effect must spill over to the extra liturgical confines and constitute a thematic agendum in the lifestyle of the assembly. A fire brand homily is both formative and informative, hopeful and optimistic and above all positive to life and its vicissitudes.If there is any thing a homily is not, it is not an occasion or forum for venting one's personal anger, a public x-ray of any person or system, or being arrogant in speech (cf. Eph. 4:29-32). Even in correcting errors or rebuking, the nature of the homily still demands prudence and edifying methodology with the ultimate intention of winning back souls for the Lord.

The best of homilies is the one which is first preached to self. A well written homily still remains the ideal for the numerous advantages it has. For instance, when written, one can say much in a little time. A written homily facilitates a good take-off and a safe landing. It curbs the irritating practice of endless repetitions. It is usually precise, *ad rem,* and gives the psychological satisfaction of being prepared and very well in control of the theme.

Being written does not necessarily mean that it has to be delivered by reading the text verbatim. A written homily convinces the homilist and the audience of exercising a serious, formal and public function, and not a casual speech or mere conversation.

Best of homilies is usually the fruit of many hours of prayer, study, reflections on the text and dexterity in application. Part of good homily lies in the art of delivery. First, it has to be delivered with very clear and distinct voice, popularly referred to as the preachers voice, and not with a bed room voice. Proper use of public address system is equally an added advantage. The same applies to the proper use of local expressions, idioms, proverbs,[215] didactic stories, literary genre and prudent use of tortoise stories[216] especially for children.

The proper use of the voice is important in the context of preaching a homily. But there is equally a need to develop the more subtle art of the liturgical use of the voice. Affectation should be avoided, but skills such as a dignity of expression and giving value to the meaning and sense of words are essential, not only for communication, but for the distinctive proclamation of public speech.[217]

# CHAPTER EIGHT

# PRACTICAL QUESTIONS ON LITURGICAL PRAXES

## Introduction

These questions often bother on the various celebrations of the church. They are often borne out of concern for what seem to be aberrations and abuses in the church's liturgy. Could it be that these abuses stem from ignorance of the church's liturgy, or non appreciation of this singular and proud legacy of the church? Sometimes the root cause of this nonchalance is traceable to the seminaries and other higher Institutes of theological studies. If liturgy is taken rather serious and given its rightful place among the priorities in the curriculum of studies and in the local churches perhaps these anomalies the church experiences today could be reduced a great deal, if not entirely eradicated.

## On the Eucharistic Celebration

1.      Some of the questions deal with the nature and dignity of the eucharistic celebration. For instance, is the celebration a sacrifice, a meal to be shared, re-enactment of the mystery of salvation *par excellence* or just mere social gathering?

2.      There are questions dealing with the structure, elements and parts of the eucharistic celebration. For instance, are celebrants free to readjust the present structure of the Mass by celebrating the kiss of peace before beginning the penitential rite?; does the first kiss of peace suffice or does one need to repeat it after the prayer following the Our Father?

3.      What should be the appropriate greeting to the assembly at the commencement of eucharistic celebration after making the sign of the Cross? Could one use one of the formulas given in the official liturgical book like the Lord be with you? or to use the common social

formula of saying, *Good Morning or Good day* as the case may be, or still the cultural formula of saying, *Ndi be anyi, nma nma nu?* For what has the assembly gathered?

Liturgy which is a public, formal and official gathering of Christ the head and members is also hierarchically structured. Liturgy is not a merely social gathering which could be either formal or casual. It admits some element of wholesome cultural values of the people and so could be socially inclined or cultic. One mad then ask, could there be any other greeting for the liturgical gathering better than ***the Lord be with you***? Could it be that the celebrant is in doubt about the theological significance of this greeting or the assembly is in doubt of it? Could it be that the celebrant finds this greeting insufficient or a meaningless empty phrase and, therefore, has to be substituted with something more social, or the assembly feels unsatisfied with being greeted as such and so would need either a substitute or augmentation? What is really wrong being greeted socially or culturally at the eucharistic celebration?

4.  What practical reasons are there for an assisting deacon to kneel from the epiclesis till after consecration? Does it not look clumsy and unrealistic?

5.  Why are the divergent gestures during the *Epiclesis* and Consecration? Should there not be a uniform agreed gesture for each of these so that there could be less distraction at a Concelebration?

6.  What about the over singing tendency especially the long choruses and clapping which seem to be the yard stick for a successful liturgical celebration. To what extent is it advisable to sing at the eucharistic celebration?

7.  What liturgical purpose does the song preceding the homily serve? Should it not come rather before the first reading as introducing the liturgy of the Word, or is the homily to be delivered by the celebrant more important than the Word of God itself? Is the commentary on the Word more significant than the Word itself?

8.  Other questions bother on gestures, gesticulations, movements and postures, especially with regard to the posture of the celebrant's hand while reciting the presidential prayers at Mass.

9. During Concelebration, for instance, who and who should extend hands to the offerings during consecration? Should it be all the priests' concelebrants and the entire assembly as some tend to do today? Among concelebrants, what distinctive posture do they maintain during the *epiclesis* and consecration? Do they maintain the same gesture at both moments or differently?

10. Of what liturgical significance is the practice of carrying the consecrated host elevated for the people *to see and adore* at the moment of consecration round the aisles of the church, the same as the consecrated wine in the chalice? Apart from merely arousing people's emotions, sentiments shown by the confused or inarticulate incantations that go with them, of what better reason are these protracted elevations?

11. What is the symbolism of elevating the consecrated host and wine? Is it for adoration of the assembly? Or to be carried through the aisles of the church for instantaneous healing amidst chaotic incantations by the assembly punctuated with hymns that are short of being eucharistic?

12. Where two priests are concelebrating privately, what is the liturgical meaning of elevating the consecrated host and wine? Has the action been reduced to mere rubricism as both stand at par facing the consecrated specie, or saying this is the lamb of God and raising the host, while both have a piece on the hand? Of what significance is raising the host at all, if not mere rubricism?

13. What about the clashing roles of eucharistic ministers? a situation whereby the ministers overstep their bounds, the scope and limits of the roles as chief celebrant, other concelebrants, deacon, acolytes, lectors, psalmists, the school of cantors, commentator and the assembly?

14. What could be responsible for a situation where the celebrant cancels out every other minister as good for nothing and does everything all alone? Two things are clear from this: it shows that the assembly is not prepared for the celebration. Second, it reduces the celebration to a-one-man show, thus making the celebration a mere spectacle where the assembly becomes simply spectators. The reformed liturgy of the

Second Vatican Council condemns this attitude as unacceptable, because it contravenes the very aim of the reforms which is active, conscious, plenary participation in the liturgy.[218]

15. Complexities arise from the proclamation of the Gospel at a Concelebration at which the bishop is present whether as celebrant or merely presiding without being the celebrant. Why should a priest for instance proclaiming the gospel in the absence of a deacon, go to the Bishop for blessing and after proclaiming the gospel, take the book of the gospel to be kissed by the bishop? Is the priest not an ordinary minister of the Word?

16. What about the complexities arising from the veneration of the Altar and the Book of the Gospel, the issue of genuflection at a Concelebration?

17. What about the variations about incensation with three swings and no longer three double swings in three places; the issue of two swings and single swing?

18. What about the liturgical symbolism attached to the lectern, the chair of the celebrant and other chairs; the place of the assembly which today seems to be muddled up? Can anyone sit wherever one wishes to?

## Liturgical Architecture

1. Are any consultations made regarding the construction of churches to the diocesan liturgy commission today against the background and principles guiding the erection of liturgical edifices and their furnishings, liturgical arts as well articulated in the second chapter above?

## Liturgical Vestments

1. What liturgical pieces of advice are being given to those who make the vestments and the sacred vessels?

2. Who is responsible for the multi-coloured, cheap and non-befitting materials and designs of the many liturgical vestments seen today?

3.     What about the arbitrary use of liturgical colours at liturgical celebrations and Concelebrations?

## Liturgical Dressing

1.     The improper dressing of putting a stole on top of a cassock or Soutane for eucharistic celebration, nay the liturgical celebrations.
2.     What about the practice of stole and chasuble on top of Soutane for eucharistic celebration, especially today when very light materials for sewing vestments abound?

## Sacred Species

1.     The liturgical elements required for the celebration of the Eucharist, how much attention does one pay to the quality of the bread, wine and water destined for liturgical celebration?
2.     When can the church in the missions think of alternative local elements, in case a situation arises where importation of these elements becomes next to impossible? Would the church in the missions cease from celebrating the Eucharist?
3.     When the corporals and purificators gather the sacred species at the end of each eucharistic celebration, what is the fate of those particles? Who takes care of them?
4.     What importance does one attach to purificators, corporals, sacrarium, sacred vessels like chalice, ciboria and paten?

## Use of Alternatives and Optionals

1.     The choice of Masses to be celebrated; the nature and dignity of the Ritual and Votive Masses; are the celebrants even aware of the existence of such variations in the liturgy, and when can they be celebrated?
2.     The use of eucharistic prayers and arbitrary choice of Masses for the dead. Are celebrants condemned to Eucharistic Prayer two, oblivious

of the existence of about ten other approved Eucharistic prayers to choose from especially the fourth one?

3. The assembly needs to be exposed to the other aspects of the history of salvation as narrated by these other eucharistic prayers.

4. It would be unreasonable to sacrifice the need for these variations on the altar of saving time. The Church must have time to worship and not merely attend to fulfil the law.


## Quality and Theological Contents of Homilies

1. One often meets such questions bothering on the quality of homilies that are being delivered today.

2. What is homily meant to be? a commentary on the Word, or an exhortation, an entertainment galore, eulogy, a singing spree punctuated with dancing and clapping?


## Lack of the sense of mystery that is being celebrated

1. How often does one realise that what one is celebrating and participating in is a mystery, filled with symbols and meaning, and so demands every consciousness of what is being done at every stage of any celebration?

2. Sometimes, the attitude one exhibits towards the liturgical celebrations indicates clearly the absence of this awareness that one is dealing with a mystery couched in symbols, and the mystery is that of salvation?

3. Who is Jesus whose mysteries one celebrates? Is he an instant God that needs an instant minister for an instant solution? A God that can be ordered around and manipulated? Is he a magical God?

4. We live in a world where people find themselves surrounded by so many problems that need to be solved instantly. People look for ministers who can provide instant answers and solutions to these problems. The ministers must consult an instant God, an automatic machine God who answers mechanically and instantly. They rush in

and soon after that they disappear. There is no continuity. Why is this kind of fast-food approach to the mysteries of salvation?

5.	Some of the ministers knowingly or unknowingly appear to offer instant solutions to these problems. Just like medicine and cure, the patients discover a deep sense of trust in their ministers, and that is already a major source of cure. Patients usually get cured when they discover a deep sense of trust and confidence in their doctor. That is the first thing a good doctor strives to establish with the patients. The more the trust the more likelihood of cure. If the doctor fails to establish that he would normally refer the patient to some other doctor. Are the ministers still in control of this confidence?

6.	Doctors discover that many patients are cured just because of little care, and some die because of much care. Doctors therefore, emphasise more preventive measures as much as curative measures, hence the adage, prevention is better than cure. Perhaps a little elaboration and a proposal may be necessary here. The work of the ordained minister is somewhat like that. If one gives the people a listening ear to their problems, they will be attracted. Establish confidence and trust in them and one finds no space to accommodate the crowd. Mention their problems in public prayer, they besiege your church. He cares for us and he prays for us will be their verdict.

## Ordained Ministers in Vicarious Status

1.	The danger some ministers run into is sometimes to forget that they are standing in for someone. Thus instead of saying: *benedicat vos* ... bless you they say *benedicat nos* ... bless us .....

2.	Why the mutilation of the prayers of the church: *sed libera nos a malo* ... but deliver us from evil, and not *sed libera nos ab omni malo* – but deliver us from all evil?

3.	Imagine the upsurge of many spiritual renewals and movements. These could be understood as positive indications of hearts seeking direction, seeking ways of expressing their yearning for God and, therefore, pose a great challenge to the liturgy the church celebrates. It becomes a great tragedy when the celebrants themselves are caught up in these trends, and thus the problem of spiritual leadership arises. How far is a given local church able to tackle this challenge?

4. The present society requires celebrants with authentic theology to offer the yearning hearts the needed satisfaction. The Bible and mysteries of Christ in the hands of poorly informed celebrants is like a child toying with an explosive weapon. How far are the present celebrants articulating this problem in the scheme of their continuous formation?

5. A little bit of interest added to the seminary formation could provide some solid base already for this apostolate. No one studies the exegesis of all the verses of the Bible. The essence of exegesis is to equip one with the tools of studying the Bible so that even on ones own one can apply the tools, have a good take off and a safe landing. How much of this interest is seen today in the celebrants?

6. The ordained minister of the Word must be very conversant with the Bible. He speaks with authority like his master. This is an area of specialisation and, therefore, the minister ought to be an authority in the mastery and delivery of the Word. What percentage can be allotted to the present day ministers of the Word?

The essence of this chapter is not simply to pin-point anomalies, abuses and aberrations. Just as it is important to raise these questions, it is equally important to find satisfactory answers to them. The answers have to be deeply theological, sufficiently spiritual, practically pastoral and authentically cultural. Liturgical questions of this nature cannot be dismissed with a wave of hands, or taken as a matter one can simply ignore or sweep under the carpet. They cannot be solved by on the spot answers either. This will invariable lead to question and answer syndrome that is characteristic of the infant Catechism.

Perhaps the best practical solution to these and many other liturgical problems is to return to the pristine state of liturgy of the historical classical period of the eighth century, when the liturgy was very well understood and admirably celebrated. It was a significant period in the history of the liturgy. Liturgical science and practice were at their highest peak. This was the period which the reformed liturgy of the Second Vatican Council feels a deep sense of nostalgia for and wishes to return to.

Faithful obedience to the new Revised General Instruction on the Roman Missal of 2001 would serve as a useful means of keeping the liturgy alive. A great deal of time for liturgical scholarship becomes inevitable, coupled with sound and seasoned liturgical praxes. Until the science and practice of liturgy is taken more seriously at various levels of the Church, the challenges of the on-going inculturation of the liturgy will continue to stare the local Churches and the nation squarely on the face.

The status and emphasis given to the liturgy in the seminaries and theological tertiary Institutions should be reviewed dispassionately and given priority where it should be. No wonder then to reform the entire life of the Church after so many years of decadence, the Council Fathers wisely began with the reformation of the worshipping forms of their members.

## Conclusion

A well celebrated liturgy brings about tremendous joy. It aims at and promotes active, conscious and plenary participation in the members. It effects the up-lifting of the mind, transformation of the individuals unto sanctification, edification of the church, and ultimate glorification of God. Celebration of the mysteries of Christ is, therefore, the primary assignment of the ordained minister in the church.

As his area of specialisation, he needs to exercise this function with the best in him. Recent developments in the area of liturgy must be reflected in his celebration as evidence of thinking and feeling with the church whom he is called to serve. On-going liturgical formation and information are necessary for him to be able to be current, and save his liturgical actions from archaism and routine syndrome.

Haphazard liturgical inculturation in any form or shape has no place in the liturgy of the church. Liturgical inculturation strongly abhors the mutilation of an already existing approved rite or text. Mere juxtaposition of new texts by adding to or subtracting from an existing text is not only unacceptable but intolerable. Mutilation of texts by the celebrant as a sign of aversion for the apparent aridity of the existing Roman rite manifests one's inner emptiness and crass ignorance of the principles of liturgical inculturation. The best way to show such an aversion is to put one's pen on paper and submit one's discoveries to the appropriate ecclesiastical authority for approval and use.

Authentic liturgical inculturation goes far beyond superficial adjustments and mutilation of an existing rite. It consists in a clearly thought out and systematised worshipping form or pattern duly studied as containing and conveying the cultural elements, values, and the genius of the people. Genuine liturgical inculturation excludes on the spot mutilation of a rite, mental colonialism and imposition.

# GENERAL CONCLUSION

To prosper and preserve the proud legacy of the church, namely the liturgy, concerted efforts are necessary, and these should be rightly channelled along the following lines. Conscientious efforts have to be made toward an authentic enrichment of the church's liturgy. The importance of enriching the liturgy with the cultural values and the genius of the people cannot be over stressed. It brings about a high level of involvement, because their contributions to the liturgy are well appreciated and formed an integral part of their worshipping form. They feel at home with the celebration, and they enjoy a greater sense of belonging.

The consequences that flow from this are quite obvious. First it enhances active, conscious, and plenary participation which forms the main aim of the reformed liturgy of the Second Vatican Council. Second, it facilitates the radical change in the thinking pattern of the people, brings about total transformation, sanctification of the people, leading to the edification of the entire church and the glorification of God.

The happy restoration of the liturgy to its pristine position remains one unique way of keeping it alive. The achievement of this singular aim of the Fathers of the Second Vatican Council, consists in evolving a liturgy that is distinguished by noble simplicity, brevity, practicality and sobriety. It includes elaborate programme of scientific research and authentic praxes.

The credits of such a renewed liturgy is that it is tailored to address the concrete concerns of the people. The practicality of the liturgy becomes rather obvious for all to witness to. The people accept this rite as their own, and then undertake to preserve and cherish it as much as possible.

# APPENDIX ONE

# NEW LITURGICAL TEXTS FOR SPECIAL
# EUCHARISTIC CELEBRATION

# (A CASE FOR NATIONAL EUCHARISTIC CONGRESS)

## Introduction

The National Eucharistic Congress always offers a wonderful opportunity of grace, blessings and challenges to the church especially when celebrated at a critical period in the socio-political life of any country. It points to the fatherly love of God who made the supreme sacrifice of his Son for the salvation of humankind. It reminds the church and society at large of what it means to love for others to live and be saved. Love is best expressed in a willing acceptance of suffering, sacrifice, service, obedience and letting-go. In the Eucharist all these virtues are exemplified for the faithful to admire and imitate.

For a meaningful celebration of the Congress, creative innovations should be proposed to save the people from the routine syndrome. These innovations are expected to take place in so many ways. Essentially these innovations should be well manifested in euchological creativity, new eucharistic hymns etc. Socially, artistic works, pamphlets, leaflets as funfair, jingles about the Congress, hand outs, hand bills, souvenirs like head ties, T-shirts, caps, etc. should be displayed as early as possible. All levels of official media, the Church, State and National should advertise the celebration as a prayerful strategy of the church to bring sanity and hope to the people. Lectures at grass-root level should be in place to give the celebration the publicity and the seriousness that it duly deserves.

# Quest For New Liturgical Texts

The need for new liturgical creativity cannot be over-emphasised. Incidentally, the out-going Roman Missal of Paul V1, which is being over taken by the *Editio typica Tersa* of the Roman Missal of 2002, does not contain any Mass formulary for celebrating Eucharistic Congresses. Except for mere adaptation of what one could find in the Missal for the Solemnity of the Body and Blood of Christ[219] and the text for the Votive Mass of the Holy Eucharist.[220] Even at that, one has only the basic five formularies of ***opening prayer, prayer over the gifts, preface, and post communion prayer*** without a specific eucharistic prayer. These go to show the deficiency in the Roman Missal. These standard texts are drawn irrespective of the particular situations of the individual local church in celebrating the Congress. This marks the inclination of the West toward uniformity which was definitively broken by the Second Vatican Council.

The Council's document *Sacrosanctum Concilium* especially nr. 37 was a calculated attempt to move away from the uniformity and rigidity that flowed from the Council of Trent. The document emphasises rather the church's openness to welcome patterns of behaviour, thoughts, gestures and rituals of diverse groups of peoples, provided these patterns are not in conflict with the faith.[221]

On very clear terms, the document insists that, even in the liturgy, the church has no wish to impose a rigid uniformity in matters which do not involve the faith or the good of the whole community. Rather she respects and fosters the spiritual adornments and gifts of the various races and peoples. Anything in their way of life that is not indissolubly bound up with superstition and error she studies with sympathy and, if possible, preserves intact. Sometimes in fact, she admits such things into the liturgy itself, as long as they harmonise with its true and authentic spirit.

The patristic principle of diversity is not only reaffirmed in the document on the liturgy, but it became further widened especially in respecting other rites like the Orientals, and perhaps other such rites as may be created by any group. These innovations the document sees as an adornment for the church and an affirmation of the divine unity in diversity to peoples of the Western rite.

The return to diversity can be realised in two ways. First there may be adaptation of the typical editions of the liturgical books of the Roman Rite to different groups provided the unity of the Roman rite is maintained.[222] Second, there may be a more radical adaptation which will involve a complete departure from the Roman pattern of liturgy to a more original form imbued with the cultural values and the genius of the people. Of these two, the Eucharistic Congress would be left to adopt a mixture of the two ways to become a third way.

The expectation here is the creation of new euchological formularies based on the Eucharist against the cultural background of the people in accordance with laid down liturgical principles. These include the *Introit Antiphon, the opening prayer, prayer over the gifts, the preface, the consecretory prayer, Communion Antiphon and Post communion prayer* as hereunder presented:

## Entrance Antiphon:  Ps. 77:23-25

He opened the gates of heaven and rained down manna for them to eat.
He gave them bread from heaven; men ate the bread of angels.

### Collect
Almighty God and Father,
the blessed and only sovereign
the King of kings and the Lord of lords,
He who alone possesses immortality and
dwells in inaccessible light;
who no man has seen or can see,
who gave us his beloved Son to be our Eucharistic meal
as a memorial of his passion, death and resurrection.

As we celebrate the great meal of his Body and Blood,
the most precious gift for the unity of the universal Church
and the entire world,

may we rise up to the challenges of a genuine and faithful ministry
of saving our dear land and the whole universe.
May we pay heed to the primacy of our interior life,
to the voice of our consciences and
become deeply eucharistic souls.
So that we may know how best to adore,
to love and to appreciate the Eucharist.

Grant this through our Lord Jesus Christ, your Son,
who lives and reigns with you in the unity of the Holy Spirit,
One God, for ever and ever.
**Amen**.

**Liturgy of the Word**               cf. Lect. Nrr. 904-909.
**First Reading: Old Testament**
**Gen. 14:18-20:** He brought bread and wine
**Ex. 16:2-4; 12-15:** I will rain down bread for you from the heavens.


## Responsorial Psalm

Ps. 109: 1-4;
**Response:**
You are a priest for ever,
a priest like Melchizedek of old,
Christ the Lord offered bread and wine.


**Ps. 77:3-4:23-25; 54. Resp. v. 24.**
**Response:**
The Lord gave them bread from heaven.


## Second Reading: New Testament

**1 Cor. 10:16-17:**
That there is only one loaf means, though there are many of us, we form a
single body.

**Heb. 9:11-15:**

The blood of Christ can purify our inner self from dead actions.

### Gospel Acclamation

Alleluia, alleluia!

He who eats my flesh and drinks my blood

lives in me and I live in him, says the Lord. Alleluia!

or

Alleluia, alleluia!

As I, who am sent by the living Father,

myself draw life from the Father,

so whoever eats me will draw life from me,

says the Lord. Alleluia!

### Gospel: Mk. 14:12-16, 22-26

This is my body. This is my blood.

or

### Jn. 6:1-15:

Jesus gave out as much as was wanted to all who were sitting ready.

### Prayer over the Gifts

Lord God,

in everything, may you be praised and glorified

especially through this bread and wine which we offer.

May our celebration of this great mystery

bring all your people peace and unity; happiness and joy.

Grant this through Christ our Lord.

**Amen.**

# Preface

The Lord be with you!
**And also with you!**

Lift up your hearts!
**We lift them up to the Lord!**

Let us give thanks to the Lord our God!
**It is right to give him thanks and praise!**

Father all-powerful and ever-living God,
we do well always and everywhere to give you thanks and praise,
through your beloved Son Jesus Christ,
the high priest of our offerings,
our protector and helper in our weakness.

**Assembly:**[223]
**Glory, honour, power and majesty, be unto God, Amen (2ice).**

Through him, you have called us from darkness to light;
from ignorance to the full knowledge of your glorious name.
He has given us the totality of his Being in the most holy sacrament of the
Eucharist, the most precious meal of his Body and Blood;
the most nourishing meal that promotes national unity and universal togetherness.

**Assembly:**
**Glory, honour, power and majesty, be unto God, Amen (2ice).**

As we eat his Body and drink his Blood:
we learn fraternal forgiveness and sincere tolerance of one another;
we truly feel the pulse of our sisters and brothers in their hunger and thirst
for material and spiritual needs;

we sincerely grow in inter-religious understanding and co-operation
with all men and women;
we courageously persevere in the dialogue of cultures and ethnic diversity;
and thus build a society that shows great respect
for the dignity of the human person.

**Assembly:**
**Glory, honour, power and majesty, be unto God, Amen (2ice).**

And so, with all the angels, saints and our ancestors,
we sing for ever the unending hymn of your praise:

**Assembly: Holy, Holy, Holy....**

## Consecretory Prayer

**Principal Celebrant (PC)**
We come to you, Almighty Father,
with praise and thanksgiving
for the abundant riches of your grace.
For when we were sinners,
you made us worthy in keeping with your great mercy
to celebrate the most holy mystery of the Body and Blood
of your Son, our Lord Jesus Christ,
our eternal high priest and most innocent victim.

Through him,
we implore you,
to strengthen us, so that we may celebrate
with perfect charity and sincere devotion,
this wonderful mystery you have entrusted to us.

**Assembly:**
**Holy, holy is the Lord! (2ice).**

**All Concelebrants:- Epiclesis!**

Heavenly Father, we humbly implore you
to send down your Holy Spirit upon this sacrifice,
(the witness of the sufferings of Jesus,)
that he may transform this bread and wine
into the Body and Blood of our Lord Jesus Christ.

**Assembly:**
**Holy, holy is the Lord! (2ice).**
**Principal Celebrant – Institution Narrative**
On the night Jesus was betrayed,
while at supper with his disciples,
he took bread in his most holy and spotless hands,
and lifting up his eyes to his heavenly Father,
he said the blessing, he broke the bread, gave it to them and said:

**All Concelebrants**

TAKE THIS ALL OF YOU AND EAT IT!
THIS IS MY BODY WHICH WILL BE GIVEN UP FOR YOU!

*At the elevation of the host for adoration and profession of faith by all, a*
*proper meditative hymn could be sung such as, O come let us adore him....,*
*without prejudice to the recommended prayerful silence.*

He also filled the cup with wine mixed with water,
he said the blessing, gave it to them and said,

TAKE THIS ALL OF YOU AND DRINK FROM IT,
THIS IS THE CUP OF MY BLOOD,
THE BLOOD OF THE NEW AND EVERLASTING COVENANT;
IT WILL BE SHED FOR YOU AND FOR ALL
SO THAT SINS MAY BE FORGIVEN.
DO THIS IN MEMORY OF ME.

*At the elevation of the chalice for adoration and profession of faith a proper meditative hymn could be sung such as O come let us adore him...., without prejudice to the recommended prayerful silence.*

**Let us proclaim the mystery of faith!**

**Assembly:**
**Christ has died,**
**Christ is risen,**
**Christ will come again!**[224]

**All Concelebrants (with hands extended): Anamnesis:**

Eternal Father,
we re-enact with praise and gratitude
the great mystery of our salvation:
the passion and death of your Son on the Cross of Calvary;
his glorious resurrection and ascension into heaven,
where he is seated at your right hand,
there interceding for us as our eternal high priest and mediator with you.
We recall the descent of the Holy Spirit as his witness,
our comforter, teacher and sanctifier;
and expecting your Son's return in glory,
when the elect will join him in happiness for ever.

**Assembly:**
**Holy, holy is the Lord! (2ice).**

**1 CC. Epiclesis of Communion**

Most generous Father,
may your Holy Spirit transform and empower all those
who take part in this sacrifice,
may they become one body, one mind and heart, and one spirit in Christ.
May they be strengthened in devotion to the glory of your name;

may they obtain forgiveness of their sins;
be delivered from the wiles of the devil,
its errors, lures and attractions, and be truly reconciled with you,
so that faithful to the Lord's command, we your people and your ministers
will continuously make present under the appearance of bread and wine,
the sacrifice of your Son truly, really and substantially;
that sacrament which has redeemed humanity from sin
and continues to reveal the hope of a future of salvation,
for the women and men of every time and place until the end of time.

**Assembly:**
**Holy, holy is the Lord! (2ice).**


## 2 CC: Intercession

Most gracious Father,
may this sacrifice bring your heavenly blessings,
peace and unity to the whole world.
Protect with your mighty power the one, holy, catholic and apostolic
Church
that is spread from one end of the world to the other;
keep her sheltered from the menace and the agitation
of materialism and strange doctrines; bigotry and fanaticism;
may she constantly rise up to the challenges
of a genuine and faithful ministry of saving the world.
May she always enjoy the grace of increasing the enthusiasm and joy
of your priesthood, consecrated life and christian activism.
May she persevere in the pursuit of dialogue of cultures, religions and eth-
nicity.

**Assembly:**
**Holy, holy is the Lord! (2ice).**

## 3 CC.

Almighty and eternal God,
May your abundant blessings
remain with all those who help us to do your will on earth:
our parents, friends and relations
those specially assigned to the work of evangelisation:
the religious women and men,
deacons and priests
our bishop................
all the bishops especially ................our Pope.
May they continually enjoy a healthy communion and
for the sake of your Church preserve them from all shame and evil,
keep them in health and honour,
long life and an honourable old age in piety and righteousness.

**Assembly:**
**Holy, holy is the Lord!**

## 4 CC.

Ever-loving Father,
we bless and glorify you
for our sisters and brothers in faith,
who have done your will on earth,
our Holy, Glorious, Immaculate and Blessed Virgin Mary,
the Mother of God and of the Church,
St. Joseph her husband, the apostles, the martyrs and saints especially,
**St. Patrick, the Second Patron of Nigeria and**
**our Blessed Brother Cyprian-Michael Iwene Tansi**
and all the just who kept the faith of Christ until the end of their life.
May we after doing your will on earth be counted among those to be chosen.

**Assembly:**
**Holy, holy is the Lord! (2ice).**

**5 CC**

Most merciful Father,
we hopefully entrust into your most loving care
the souls of our departed sisters and brothers.
They trust in your mercy with the hope of resurrection,
when you will admit them into your kingdom.
With confidence in your fatherly love,
we shall re-unite with them in your heavenly presence,
seeing you our God face to face as you are.

**CC: – doxology**
**Through him,**
**with him,**
**in him,**
**in the unity of the Holy Spirit,**
**all glory and honour is yours**
**almighty Father, for ever and ever.**
**Assembly: Amen!**

## Communion Antiphon

I am the living bread from heaven, says the Lord. If anyone eats this bread
he will live for ever; the bread I shall give is my flesh for the life of the
world.

## Prayer After Communion:

Lord God,
we have shared in the Body and Blood of your beloved Son, Jesus
Christ. May this communion foster our permanent communion
with you and with peoples of all races, religions, cultures and
colours. May it promote unity, healing and harmony in our diversity; and recognition of the variety of our spiritual gifts and min-

istries. At the end may we come to enjoy that eternal bliss with you in heaven, where you live and reign for ever and ever.

**Assembly: Amen!**

# APPENDIX TWO

# THIRD NATIONAL EUCHARISTIC CONGRESS

(with the Assembly's interjection only at the prayer of consecration)

### Entrance Antiphon    Ps. 77:23-25

He opened the gates of heaven and rained down manna for them to eat.
He gave them bread from heaven; men ate the bread of angels.

### Collect
Almighty God and Father,
the blessed and only sovereign
the King of kings and the Lord of lords,
He who alone possesses immortality and
dwells in inaccessible light;
whom no man has seen or can see,
who gave us his beloved Son to be our Eucharistic meal
as a memorial of his passion, death and resurrection.

As we celebrate the great meal of his Body and Blood,
the most precious gift for the unity of the universal Church and
the entire world, may we rise up to the challenges of a genuine
and faithful ministry of saving our dear country and the whole
universe.
May we pay heed to the primacy of the interior life,
to the voice of our consciences and become
deeply eucharistic souls.
So that we may know how to adore, love and enjoy the Eucharist.

Grant this through our Lord Jesus Christ, your Son, who lives and reigns with you in the unity of the Holy Spirit, One God, for ever and ever.

**Amen.**

## Liturgy of the Word                    Lect. Nrr. 904-909.

### First Reading: Old Testament

**Gen. 14:18-20:** He brought bread and wine.

**Ex. 16:2-4; 12-15:** I will rain down bread for you from the heavens.

### Responsorial Psalm

Ps. 109: 1-4;

### Response

You are a priest for ever,
a priest like Melchizedek of old,
Christ the Lord offered bread and wine.

**Ps. 77:3-4:23-25; 54. Resp. v. 24.**

### Response:

The Lord gave them bread from heaven.

## Second Reading: New Testament

### 1 Cor. 10:16-17:

That there is only one loaf means, though there are many of us, we form a single body.

### Heb. 9:11-15:

The blood of Christ can purify our inner self from dead actions.

## Gospel Acclamation

Alleluia, alleluia!
He who eats my flesh and drinks my blood
lives in me and I live in him, says the Lord.
Alleluia!

## Gospel: Mk. 14:12-16, 22-26
This is my body. This is my blood.

## Gospel Acclamation
**Alleluia, alleluia!**
As I, who am sent by the living Father,
myself draw life from the Father,
so whoever eats me will draw life from me,
says the Lord. Alleluia!

# Gospel: Jn. 6:1-15:

Jesus gave out as much as was wanted to all who were sitting ready.

## Prayer over the Gifts
Lord God,
in everything, may you be glorified
especially through this bread and wine which we offer.
May our celebration of this great mystery
bring all your people peace, unity, happiness and joy.
Grant this through Christ our Lord.

**Amen.**

**Preface**
The Lord be with you!
**And also with you!**
Lift up your hearts!

**We have lifted them up to the Lord!**
Let us give thanks to the Lord our God!
**It is right to give him thanks and praise!**

Father all-powerful and ever-living God,
we do well always and everywhere to give you thanks and praise,
through your beloved Son Jesus Christ, the high priest of our offerings,
our protector and helper in our weakness.

Through him, you have called us from darkness to light;
from ignorance to the full knowledge of your glorious name.
He has given us the totality of his Being in the most holy sacrament of the
Eucharist,
the most precious meal of his Body and Blood;
the most nourishing meal that promotes national unity and universal togetherness.

As we eat his Body and drink his Blood:
we learn fraternal forgiveness and sincere tolerance of one another;
we truly feel the pulse of our sisters and brothers in their hunger and thirst
for material and spiritual needs;
We sincerely grow in inter-religious understanding and co-operation
with all men and women;
we courageously persevere in the dialogue of cultures and ethnic diversities;
and thus build a society that shows great respect
for the dignity of the human person.

And so, with all the angels, saints and our ancestors,
we sing for ever, the unending hymn of your praise singing:

**Assembly: Holy, Holy, Holy....**

# Consecratory Prayer

**Principal Celebrant:**

We come to you, Almighty Father,
with praise and thanksgiving
for the abundant riches of your grace.
For when we were sinners,
you made us worthy in keeping with your great mercy
to celebrate the most holy mystery of the Body and Blood
of your Son, our Lord Jesus Christ,
our eternal high priest and most innocent victim.

Through him,
we implore you,
to strengthen us, so that we may celebrate
with perfect charity and sincere devotion,
this wonderful mystery you have entrusted to us.

**Assembly:**
**Holy, holy is the Lord! (2ice).**

**All Concelebrants:- Epiclesis!**

Heavenly Father, we humbly implore you
to send down your Holy Spirit upon this sacrifice,
(the witness of the sufferings of Jesus,)
that he may transform this bread and wine
into the Body and Blood of our Lord Jesus Christ.
**Assembly:**

**Holy, holy is the Lord! (2ice).**

**Principal Celebrant – Institution Narrative**

On the night Jesus was betrayed,
while at supper with his disciples,
he took bread in his most holy and spotless hands,

and lifting up his eyes to his heavenly Father,
he said the blessing, he broke the bread, gave it to them and said:

**All Concelebrants**
TAKE THIS ALL OF YOU AND EAT IT!
THIS IS MY BODY WHICH WILL BE GIVEN UP FOR YOU!

*At the elevation of the host for adoration and profession of faith by all, a
proper meditative hymn could be sung such as, O come let us adore him....,
without prejudice to the recommended prayerful silence.*

He also filled the cup with wine mixed with water,
he said the blessing, gave it to them and said,

TAKE THIS ALL OF YOU AND DRINK FROM IT,
THIS IS THE CUP OF MY BLOOD,
THE BLOOD OF THE NEW AND EVERLASTING COVENANT;
IT WILL BE SHED FOR YOU AND FOR ALL
SO THAT SINS MAY BE FORGIVEN.
DO THIS IN MEMORY OF ME.

*At the elevation of the chalice for adoration and profession of faith a
proper meditative hymn could be sung such as O come let us adore him....,
without prejudice to the recommended prayerful silence.*
*Let us proclaim the mystery of faith!*
**Assembly:**
**Christ has died,**
**Christ is risen,**
**Christ will come again!**

**All Concelebrants (with hands extended): Anamnesis:**
Eternal Father,
we re-enact with praise and gratitude
the great mystery of our salvation:
the passion and death of your Son on the Cross of Calvary;

his glorious resurrection and ascension into heaven,
where he is seated at your right hand,
there interceding for us as our eternal high priest and mediator with you.
we recall the descent of the Holy Spirit as his witness,
our comforter, teacher and sanctifier;
and expecting your Son's return in glory,
when the elect will join him in happiness for ever.
**Assembly:**
**Holy, holy is the Lord! (2ice).**

### 1 CC. Epiclesis of Communion

Most generous Father,
may your Holy Spirit transform and empower
all those who take part in this sacrifice,
may they become one body, one mind and heart, and one spirit in Christ.
May they be strengthened in devotion to the glory of your name;
may they obtain forgiveness of their sins;
be delivered from the wiles of the devil,
its errors, lures and attractions, and be truly reconciled with you.
so that faithful to the Lord's command, we your people and your ministers
will continuously make present under the appearance of bread and wine,
the sacrifice of your Son truly, really and substantially;
that sacrament which has redeemed humanity from sin
and continues to reveal the hope of a future of salvation,
for the women and men of every time and place until the end of time.

**Assembly:**
**Holy, holy is the Lord! (2ice).**

### 2 CC: Intercession

Most gracious Father,
may this sacrifice bring your heavenly blessings,
peace and unity to the whole world.
Protect with your mighty power the one, holy, catholic and apostolic
Church

that is spread from one end of the world to the other;
keep her sheltered from the menace and the agitation
of materialism and strange doctrines; bigotry and fanaticism;
may she constantly rise up to the challenges
of a genuine and faithful ministry of saving the world.
May she always enjoy the grace of increasing the enthusiasm and joy
of your priesthood, consecrated life and christian activism.
May she persevere in the pursuit of dialogue of cultures, religions and eth-
nicity.

**Assembly:**
**Holy, holy is the Lord! (2ice).**

**3 CC.**
Almighty and eternal God,
May your abundant blessings
remain with all those who help us to do your will on earth:
our parents, friends and relations
those specially assigned to the work of evangelisation:
the religious women and men,
deacons and priests
our bishop................
all the bishops especially ...............our Pope.
May they continually enjoy a healthy communion and
for the sake of your Church preserve them from all shame and evil,
keep them in health and honour,
long life and an honourable old age in piety and righteousness.

**Assembly:**
**Holy, holy is the Lord!**

**4 CC.**
Ever-loving Father,
we bless and glorify you
for our sisters and brothers in faith,

who have done your will on earth,
our Holy, Glorious, Immaculate and Blessed Virgin Mary,
the Mother of God and of the Church,
St. Joseph her husband, the apostles, the martyrs and saints especially,
**St. Patrick, the Second Patron of Nigeria and**
**our Blessed Brother Cyprian-Michael Iwene Tansi**
and all the just who kept the faith of Christ until the end of their life.
May we after doing your will on earth be counted among those to be chosen.

**Assembly:**
**Holy, holy is the Lord! (2ice).**

## 5 CC

Most merciful Father,
we hopefully entrust into your most loving care
the souls of our departed sisters and brothers.
They trust in your mercy with the hope of resurrection,
when you will admit them into your kingdom.
With confidence in your fatherly love,
we shall re-unite with them in your heavenly presence,
seeing you our God face to face as you are.

**CC:**
**Through him,**
**with him,**
**in him,**
**in the unity of the Holy Spirit,**
**all glory and honour is yours**
**almighty Father, for ever and even.**

**Assembly: Amen!**

# Communion Antiphon

I am the living bread from heaven, says the Lord. If anyone eats this bread he will live for ever; the bread I shall give is my flesh for the life of the world.

**Prayer After Communion:**

Lord God,
we have shared in the Body and Blood of your beloved Son, Jesus Christ.
May this communion foster our permanent communion with you and with peoples of all races, religions, cultures and colours.
May it promote unity, healing, harmony in our diversities;
and recognising the variety of our spiritual gifts and ministries.
At the end may we come to enjoy that eternal bliss with you in heaven, where you live and reign for ever and ever.

**Assembly: Amen!**

# NOTES

## General Introduction

1 *Document on the Sacred Liturgy, Sacrosanctum Concilium* nr. 15 (hence forth SC.).

2 SC. nr. 16.

3 Cf. Mark Searle, *Liturgy Made Simple*, The Liturgical Press, Collegeville Minnesota, p. 11-12.

## Chapter One: Notion of the Liturgy

4 Cf. *Catechism of the Catholic Church*, Paulines/St. Pauls, Libreria Editrice Vaticana, 1994, nr.1067. (Henceforth *CCC*).

5 Cf. SC. nr. 2.

6 Cf. Pope Pius X11, *Mediator Dei, AAS* 39 (1947) pp. 547-572.

7 *SC.* nr.7.

8 In the very sense in which he is both the priest and victim; the offerer and the offered, the immolator and the immolated, the oblator and the oblated.

9 Cf. *SC.* nr. 7.

10 Cf. *CCC.* nr. 1073.

11 Cf. *Ibid.* nr. 10.

12 Cf. *SC.* nr. 9.

13 Cf. *CCC.* nr. 1072.

14 Cf. Lk. 1:23; Acts 13:2; Rom. 15:16,27; 2 Cor. 9:12; Phil. 2:14-17; 25, 30.

15 Cf. Kevin W. Irwin, *Liturgical Theology, A Primer*, The Liturgical Press, Collegeville, Minnesota, 1990, p. 18.

16 Cf. *Ibid.*

17 Cf. *Ibid.* p. 19.

18 Cf. I. Dalmais, *Introduction to the Liturgy*, (trans. Roger Capel) Heilicon Publishers, Baltimore, 1961; Part 1, p. 27-95; Part 2, p. 99-197.

19 Cf. *Ibid.*, nr. 1074.

20 *Ibid.*, in his article, *La liturgie comme lieu theologique, La Maison Dieu* 78(1964) 97-106.

21 Cf. *Ibid.*, 102-104.

22 Cf. Cipriano Vagaggini, *Theological Dimensions of the Liturgy, A General Treatise on the Theology of the Liturgy,* (trans. Leonard J. Doyle and W. A. Jurgens from the 4th Italian Edition, The Liturgical Press, Collegeville-Minnesota, 1976, p. 512-514. For a thorough review of the different kinds of liturgical witnesses and how to approach their interpretation, cf. M. Auge, *Principi di interpretatione dei testi liturgici, Anamnesis 1., La liturgia. Momento nella storia della salvezza,* eds. B. Neunheuser et al, Marietti, Casale Monferato, 1974, 159-179.

23 Cf. *Ibid.*, p. 513-517.

24 Instances of how Marsili understood liturgical theology as he applied his method are found in the following two posthmous publications by the author: Salvatore Marsili, *Mistero di Cristo e Liturgia nello Spirito,* Libreria Editrice Vaticana, Citta del Vaticano, 1986; *Ibid., Teologia Liturgica die Sacramenti,* Edizione Liturgiche, Roma, 1987.

25 Cf. S. Marsili, *Verso una Teologia della Liturgia, Anamnesis,* 1, 47-48.

26 Cf. *Ibid.*, p. 102.

27 Cf. *Ibid, Teologia Liturgica,* 1515-19.

28 Cf Gerard Lukken, *The Unique Expression of Faith in the Liturgy, Liturgical Expression of Faith, Concilium* 82, eds. H. Schmidt and D. Power, trans. David Smith Herder and Herder, New York, 1973, 16.

29 Cf. Kevin W. Irwin, *Liturgical Theology,* p. 40-44.

30 Cf. Aidan Kavanagh, *On Liturgical Theology,* Pueblo, New York, 1984, pp. 7-102.

31 Cf. *Ibid.*

## Chapter Two: Ready To Build A Church: Practical Guide

32 Cf. *The Roman Missal,* reformed by decree of the Second Vatican Ecumenical Council, published by authority of Pope Paul VI, revised at the direction of Pope John Paul II, *Institutio Generalis Missalis Romani,* July 2000, (Henceforth *RGIRM),* nr. 288, cf. also *SC.,* art.122-124; *Presbyterorum Ordinis,* nr. 5; *Inter Oecumenici* nr. 90: *Acta Apostolicae Sedis* (henceforth *AAS*) 56 (1964), p. 897; *Eucharistici Mystici,* nr. 24: *AAS* 59(1967), p. 554.

33 Cf. *RGIRM* nr. 293.

34 Cf. Cf. Peter J. Elliott, *Ceremonies of the Modern Roman Rite, The Eucharist and the Liturgy of the Hours,* Ignatius Press, San Francisco, 1995 (henceforth *CMRR*); nr. 86.

35 Everything good comes from the East:
   i.     the patient Job came from the East;

ii. the sun rises from the East;

iii. Christ came from the East

iv. the Magi came from the East

v. ideally, the object of turning East is to face God and His only Begotten Son, who like the Sun, are thought of as enthroned in the East and coming from the East. This coming or Advent of God in His Theophany takes place on the Altar of sacrifice. Hence in a Christian Church, the object of turning East for prayer is to face the Altar, and therefore, both priest and the assembly have to turn towards the Altar. This is most probably the reason for reverting to the priest facing the people with the Altar between himself and the people as instructed by the reformed liturgy of the Second Vatican Council.

36    Cf. *RGIRM* nr. 298.

37    Cf. *CMRR*, nr. 50; cf. also *GIRM* of 1975, nr.258. It must be very spacious in cathedrals; cf. also *RGIRM* nr. 295; *Inter Oecumenici*, nr. 91: *AAS* 56(1964), p. 898.

38    The Awka Diocesan Liturgy and Inculturation Commission in their practical but systematic instructions on Church building entitled, *About to Build -- Church Design and Furnishing*, March 2003 deserves a warm congratulation. In most areas their findings are already contained in this write up. However, in a few areas where one discovers some innovations, these will obviously be incorporated with due acknowledgement (henceforth ADLIC), p. 6-7.

39    Cf. *RGIRM, CMRR*, nr. 50.

40    Cf. 1Pet. 2:4; Eph. 2:20.

41    Cf. *RGIRM* nr. 298

42    Cf. *Codex Iudex Canonici* (*CIC*) Canons 1235-6; cf. also *GIRM* of 1975, nr. 263; cf. *Ceremonial of Bishops*, (*CB*) nr. 919. Wood or metal are usual alternatives, noting that the substructure may be of stone or of the approved solid and fitting material.

43    Cf. *RGIRM* nr. 301.

44    Cf. *CIC, Canon* 1237 para. 1; *GIRM* nr. 265; *CB* nr. 923.

45    Cf. *RGIRM* nr.303.

46    Cf. *Ibid.*, nr. *CMRR* nr. 60, p. 23.cf. *RGIRM* nr.302.

47    Cf. *RGIRM* nr. 304. For more details see Ibid., nrr. 305-308.

48    *CMRR*, nr. 63.

49    Cf. *Book of Blessings, Blessing of a Cross*, nr. 1235.

50    Cf. *CMRR*, nr. 64.

51    Cf. *ADLIC*, p. 7b.

52    Cf. *Ibid.*

53    Cf. *CMRR* nr. 79.

54    Cf. *Ibid.*, nr. 80.

55    Cf. *Ibid.*, nr. 81.

56    Cf. *Ibid.*, nr. 82.

57    Cf. *Ibid.* nr. 83.

58    Cf. *Ibid.*

59    Cf. *General Introduction to Christian Initiation – per initiationis Christianae,* June 24, 1973, nr. 25.

60    Cf. Canon 938, *RGIRM* nr. 314, cf. also *Eucharistici mystici* nr. 54: *AAS* 59(1967), p. 568; cf. *Inter Ecumenici* nr. 95: *AAS* 56 (1964), p. 898.

61    Cf. *RGIRM* nr. 314.

62    The relevant directives leading up to this Canon are as follow:

     i.    Sacred Congregation for Rites, *Inter Oecuminici*, 1964, nr.95.

     ii.    Sacred Congregation for Rites, *Eucharisticum Mysterium*, 1967, nr. 53.

     iii.    *General Instruction on the Roman Missal*, 1969, nr.276.

     iv.    Sacred Congregation for Divine Worship, *Holy Communion and Worship of the Eucharist outside Mass, Introduction,* 1973, nr. 9.

     v.    Sacred Congregation for the Sacraments and Divine Worship, *Inaestimabile Donum,* 1980, nr. 24.

63    See Appendix ix in *CMRR*: nr. 888, p. 330.

64    Cf. *Ibid.*, nr. 889, p.330.

65    Cf. *Ibid.*, nr. 890, p. 330-331.

66    Cf. *Ibid.*, nr. 891, p. 331.

67    Cf. *RGIRM*, nr. 315.

68    Cf. *Ibid.*, nr. 316.

69    Cf. *GIRM* nr. 272. Ambo is a more traditional and sacral term.

70    Cf. *RGIRM* nr. 309.

71    Cf. *CMRR*, nr. 52.

72    Cf. *Ibid.*, nr. 53.

73    Cf. *GIRM* nr. 271. It should also be designed so that the back of the celebrant's chasuble need not be crushed when he is seated.

74    Cf. *RGIRM* nr. 310.

75    Cf. *GIRM* nr. 271; cf. also, *Ceremonial of Bishops,* revised by decree of the Second Vatican Ecumenical Council and published by authority of Pope John Paul 11, the Liturgical Press, Collegeville, Minnesota, 1989 nr. 50 (henceforth *CB*); But the servers should not sit on steps. Except in the context of an abbot's liturgy in his own community, this custom can give a servile or childish impression.

76    Cf. *CMRR* nr. 55.

77    Cf. *Ibid.*, nr. 56.

78    Cf. *Ibid.*, nr. 45.

79  Cf. *RGIRM* nr. 311a.
80  Kneeling is part of Catholic tradition of worship, based on the New Testament (Luke 22:41, Acts 9:40; 20:36, 21:5). To make it difficult to kneel destroys a liturgical right of the faithful and undermines the freedom of their private devotion at other times. Also, children in a family group would be unable to the altar see when everyone stands.
81  Cf. *Ibid.,* nr. 311b.
82  Cf. *Ibid.,* nr. 312.
83  Cf. *Ibid.,* nr. 313. For more detailed use of the instruments cf. nr. 313 bc.
84  Cf. *CMRR* nr. 46b.
85  Cf. *Ibid.,* nr. 47.
86  Cf. *CIC*, Canon 964 para. 2. A curtain is also useful.
87  Cf. *Ibid.,* nr. 48.
88  Cf. *CB* nr. 864.
89  Cf. *CMRR,* nr. 49.
90  In some cases permanent provision is made for them. But due to some other ulterior motives like over commercialisation and unbridled competition, they have overstepped their permanent positions to constitute themselves objects of distraction and even irritate the assembly by blocking their view.
91  Cf. *ADLIC* p. 15.
92  Cf. *CB.,* nr. 1023.
93  Cf. *ADLIC* p. 16.
94  Cf. *Ibid.*
95  Cf. *Ibid.*
96  Cf. *Ibid.*
97  Cf. *Ibid.*
98  Cf. *Ibid.*
99  Cf. *CMRR.* nr. 85a.
100  Cf. Ibid. nr. 85b.
101  Cf. *ADLIC* p. 17.
102  Cf. *Ibid.*
103  Cf. *CMRR*, nr.84; cf. also *CB.,* nr. 921, apparently to avoid the impression that Mass is offered to the saint. However, obviously this need not preclude a window depicting events from the life of that saint. Existing side altars need not be modified.
104  In the above pages of this write up are contained practical guiding principles for designing and building a Church in the spirit of the reformed liturgy of the Second Vatican Council being a reviewed document on this subject as enunciated in Appendix ii, of Theodore Klauser, *A Short History of the Western Liturgy, An Ac-*

*count and Some Reflections*, Second Edition, Oxford University Press, Oxford, 1979, pp. 161-169.

## Chapter Three: Inculturated Eucharistic Liturgy: A Proposal

105    Elochukwu E. Uzukwu, *Worship As Body Language, Introduction to Christian Worship: An African Orientation*, A Pueblo Book, The Liturgical Press, Collegeville, Minnesota, 1997, p. 273.

106    *Institutio Generalis Missalis Romani (General Instruction On The Roman Missal)* reformed by decree of the Second Vatican Ecumenical Council, published by authority of Pope Paul VI revised at the direction of Pope John Paul II, An English Language Study Translation by the Secretariat for the Liturgy of the National Conference of the Catholic Bishops, U.S.A., July 2000, nr. 73. (Henceforth *IGMR*, 2000).

107    E. E. Uzukwu, *Worship As Body Language,...*p.273.

108    Cf. *SC nrr.* 37-40 for the general principles of liturgical inculturation, the liberality, flexibility and pluralistic tendency of the reformed liturgy of the Second Vatican Council. These numbers should be read against the background of *SC.* 21; 23-24.

109    Cf. *Norme Universales de Anno Liturgico et de Calendario, Missale Romanum,* ex decreto sacrosancti oecumenici Concilii Vaticani II, instauratum auctoritate Pauli PP. VI, Editio Typica, Libreria Editrice Vaticana, 1975, nr.45; Cf. also the idea expressed in: *Documents on the Liturgy, 1963-1979, Conciliar, Papal and Curial Texts,*

110    The Order of Mass, *The Reform of the Liturgy, 1948-1975,* Matthew J. O'Connell, trans., The Liturgical Press, Collegeville, Minnesota, p.337-392.

111    Cf. Ansgar J. Chupungco, *Liturgies of the Future, The Process and Methods of Inculturation,* Paulist Press, New York, 1989, p.64.

112    Pope Paul VI, *Apostolic Constitution, Missale Romanum,* Vatican City, 1975, p. 16.

113    Cf. A. J. Chupungco, *Liturgies of the Future,....*p. 65.

114    Cf. *Ibid.*

115    Cf. *IGRM,* 2000, nrr. 207a, 311-313.

116    The first impression one gets from any Church begins with the ushers. They act as the public relations officers of any Church and so, they should have a welcoming attitude to people especially to those coming to the Church for the first time. First impression they say matters a lot.

117    Cf. *Presbyterorum Ordinis (henceforth P. O.), Decree on Priestly Ministry and Life),* nr. 5; *SC.*33; *IGMR.* nr.27.

174

118  Cf. A. M. Triacca, *The Holy Spirit*, in: *The New Dictionary of Liturgy*, D. Sartore and A. M. Triacca, eds., Edizione Paoline, Roma, Second Edition, 1984, p.1405.

119  This could well help to inform the answer as to when does the Eucharistic celebration start: The Eucharist can be safely said to start at the very moment people decide to come together to celebrate God's love, cf. Erasto J. Fernandez, *The Eucharist Step by Step*, St. Paul's Press, Bombay, 1994, p. 11.

120  Cf. Patrick C. Chibuko, *Igbo Christian Rite of Marriage, A Proposed Rite for Study and Celebration*, Peter Lang, Frankfurt am Main, 1999, p. 67.

121  Cf. Dom Gregory Dix, *The Shape of the Liturgy*, A&C Black, London, p. 414ff.

122  Cf. Lawrence Madubuko, *Towards An African Eucharistic Liturgy*, in: *Bigard Theological Studies*, July-December, 1998, vol. 18, nr. 2. p. 5-27.

123  Cf. Ibid.

124  Cf. Elochukwu E. Uzukwu, *Worship As Body Language*....p. 53, 280.

125. Cf. F. A. Arinze, *Sacrifice In Ibo Religion*, Ibadan University Press, Ibadan, 1970, reprinted 1978, p. 50.

126  E. E. Uzukwu in his work *Igbo Spirituality As Revealed Through Igbo Prayers* spoke about the first four, while E. I. Ifesie increased the list to six in his work, *Religion At The Grassroots*, p. 112-113.

127  Cf. Lawrence Madubuko, *Towards An African Eucharistic Liturgy*,....p.23.

128  Cf. Ibid., p. 23.

129  Cf. Ibid., p. 24.

130  Cf. Lucien Deiss, *The Mass*..., p. 25.

131  Cf. G. I. nr. 43.

132  Cf. *RGIRM*, nr. 88.

133  Cf. L. Deiss, *The Mass*..., p. 43.

## Chapter Four: Announcements and Extra Collections

134  A visiting priest was once confronted after Mass by some parishioners who were filled with joyful amassment to explain the new eucharistic prayer he used at a Sunday Mass. He told them that it was the fourth eucharistic prayer which has been there since the Second Vatican Council. They confessed that they never heard it before. They never knew that there was another prayer outside the short one they are given to hear each time at their parish Mass.

135  *Presbyterorum Ordinis* (*Decree on Priestly Ministry and Life*), nr. 5.

136  *Lumen Gentium*, (*Constitution on the Church*), nr. 11.

137  *Christus Dominus*, (*Decree on the Pastoral Charge of Bishops*), nr. 30.

138  Cf. SC. nr. 7.

139 Although in the same way, if Moses had attended the Last Supper of Jesus, would he likewise not have had difficulty recognising the Pasch that he used to celebrate. Cf. Lucien Deiss, *The Mass*, A Liturgical Press Book, The Liturgical Press, Collegeville, Minnesota, 1998, p. 9.

140 Justin was said to have been born at Flavia Neapolis, a pagan Roman city in the heart of Galilee. Although he lived so close to the well where Jesus had promised the Samaritan woman the living water that slakes thirst forever and leaps up for eternal life, he was ignorant of Christ. His soul thirsting for God, he set out to search the world for the truth. After series of four disappointments in the search for the truth, he finally met Christ. He was dazzled and spellbound. He said, a fire was suddenly kindled in my soul. I fell in love with the prophets and these men who had loved Christ; I reflected on all their words and found that this philosophy alone was true and profitable. That is how and why I became a philosopher. And I wish that everyone felt the same way that I do. cf. *Dialogus cum Tryphone*, 8, *Patrologia Greca* ( Hence forth, *PG*) 6:49.

At the same time he met Christ, Justin also met Christians. The life of the disciples seemed to him worthy of their Master, and their splendid scorn for death completely refuted the spiteful accusations spread against them: In the days when the teachings of Plato were my delight, I myself used to hear the accusations levelled against Christians. But when I saw how fearless they were in the face of death and of every possible terror, I realised they could not possibly be living vicious, pleasure-seeking lives. For if a man loves pleasure and debauchery, if his delight is to eat human flesh, will he seek out death, which deprives you of all these pleasures? Will he not endeavour to preserve his present life at any cost and to elude the magistrates rather than to inform on himself and be handed over to death. Cf. *Apologia* 11 12 (*PG* 6:464 AB).

After his conversion, which in all probability occurred at Ephesus about AD 130, he one again set out on his journey as a wandering philosopher. He came to Rome during the reign of Antonius Pius (138-161) and opened a christian school there. He died a martyr between 156 and 166. How moving are these words he wrote before dying! They form the most beautiful possible signature to his work: No one believes in Socrates to the point of dying for what he taught.... But for the sake of Christ not only philosophers and scholars but even workmen and uneducated people have scorned fame, fear, and death. Cf. *Apologia*, 11 10, (*PG* 6: 461 AB).

141 The Lord's Day would be Sunday in English and the other Germanic languages-Sonntag; it would be *dimanche* (French), *domenica* (Italian) *domingo* (Spanish), *Mbosi Uka* (Igbo-Nigeria).

142 The Mass as described by Justin already contains the essential components of the Christian celebration: reading of the word of God, homily of the celebrant, common prayer, and Eucharist (and second collection or extra collection apart from bread and wine and water).

143 In the early Church the normal posture for prayer was standing. This was more than an attitude of respect for God, more even than a simple inheritance from the Jewish tradition. It was, before all else, an expression of the holy freedom the Lord had given his followers by his resurrection. It was also a sign of expectation of the Lord's coming (Lk. 21:36; this expectation was especially keen on Sunday, the day that was a kind of anticipation of the eternal Day of God. Basil the Great says in his *De Sancto Spiritu* (ed. B. Pruche, SC 17bis; Paris, 1968: We pray standing on the first day of the week (Sunday).... We do so because we are risen with Christ and must seek the things that are above (Col. 3:1); therefore on the say consecrated to the resurrection, by standing when we pray we call to mind the grace given to us. But we also stand because Sunday is a kind of image of the world to come, p. 484.

144 The celebrant freely improvises the prayer of the anaphora, but in doing so he follows a basic schema.

145 That is, Friday, the eve of Saturn's day, "our present day Saturday.

146 Justin Martyr, *Apologia* 1, 67, PG. 6, 429 and 432.

147 Cf. *Catechism of the Catholic Church*, nr. 2177.

148 Cf. Ibid., nr. 2181.

149 Cf. Ibid., nr. 2182.

150 Cf. *Gaudium et Spes*, nr. 67 para. 2.

151 Cf. *SC.* nr. 7 para. 2.

152 Cf. *SC.* nr. 14.

153 Cf. *SC.* nr. 34.


## Chapter Five: Evangelisation ....

154 One reads the numerous works published on Evangelisation especially by the recent Popes as follows:

i.    the magnanimous principle of Aggiornamento initiated by Pope John XXIII that ultimately gave rise to the Second Vatican Council, especially the decree on Missionary Activity *Ad Gentes*; *Gaudium et Spes,* nr.62ff.

ii.    the Apostolic Exhortation of Paul VI, *Evangelii Nuntiandi*, 1975, nrr.75-80;79;82 which serves as the *Magna Charta* of Evangelisation, nr. 2ff.,

iii.    John Paul II, *Redemptoris Missio*, nrr.2-3; 21;25; 33-34; 49 86-87;92ff.

iv.    Pope John Paul II, Visit to Nigeria, 1982.

v. The African Synod, Rome, 1994.

vi. Pope John Paul 11, *Christi Fideles Laici,*

vii. *The Post Synodal Exhortation, Ecclesia in Africa,* 1995.

155 These include:

i. Evangelisation 2000 and *Lumen* 2000, Rome

ii. Schools of Evangelisation in Nigeria 1989-1996;

iii. Emmaus School of Evangelisation, Issele-Uku

iv. St. Paul's International Institute of Evangelisation, Emene, Enugu, 2001 to mention only a few.

156 Cf. Richard W. Chilson, *Evangelisation Homily Hints, A Source For Catholic Preachers,* Paulist Press, Mahwah, N. J. 2000, p. 4.

157 The importance of a state recognised Institute with its certificates cannot be over-emphasised: the products must be armed with a meal-ticket, not feel inferior before their counterparts like BTH holders from CIWA, not feel unwanted, redundant, inferior etc. A situation like this makes the Gospel odious and inferior unless they are priests and religious sisters and brothers who have already a definite function. One does not see how someone without a recognised certificate can be contented after four years studies; look after himself or herself with a family, or as a religious make genuine contribution to the congregation.

158 Cf. Richard W. Chilson, *Evangelisation....,* p. 6.

159 *Ibid.,* p. 7.

160 Ibid., p. 8.

161 Cf. Sherman E. Johnson, *The Gospel According to St. Matthew, Introduction and Exegesis,* in: Nolan B. Harmon, ed. *The Interpreter's Bible,* Abingdon Press, Nashville, 1987, vol. V11, pp.231-625, esp. 620.

162 Cf. Lk. 24:47-48.

163 Cf. Jn. 20:23.

164 Power simply means ability to do or act.

165 Authority means legal power, constituted power, delegated power.

166 Cf. Jn. 1: 14: *...and the Word took flesh and dwelt among us;* Phil. 2:6-12: *Jesus did not count his equality with God a thing to be grasped, he emptied himself...*

167 George A Buttrick, *The Gospel According to St. Matthew, Exposition,* in Nolan B. Harmon, ed., The Interpreter's Bible....p.622-633.

168 Cf. Leslie F. Church, ed. *Matthew Henry's Commentary on the Whole Bible in One Volume: Genesis to Revelation,* Marshall Morgan and Scott, 1960, p. 160.

169 Cf. *Ibid.*

170 Cf. Ibid.

171 Cf. *Ibid.*

172 Cf. Matt. 16:16.

173   Cf. Jn. 20:28.

174   Cf. Leslie F. Church, ed., *Matthew Henry's Commentary on the Whole Bible in One Volume*, ... p. 160.

175   Cf. Matt. 28: 20.

176   Cf. Jn. 116:7.

177   Cf. Jn. 14 : 15.
      Chapter Six: Liturgical Gestures.....

178   Cf. *SC*. nr. 116

179   Cf. *Institutio Generalis Missalis Romani* July 2000, *The Roman Missal* Reformed by Decree of the Second Vatican Ecumenical Council, published by authority of Pope Paul VI revised at the direction of Pope John Paul 11, An English Language Study Translation by the Secretariat for the Liturgy of the National Conference of Catholic Bishops, USA, SNAAP Press, Enugu, 2001, nr. 42 (henceforth RGIRM).

180   Cf. *Ibid.*

181   Cf. *Ibid.*, nr. 43a.

182   Peter Elliot, *Ceremonies of the Modern Roman Rite, The Eucharist and the Liturgy of the Hours*, Ignatius Press, San Francisco, 1995, nr. 187, p. 69.

183   Cf. *Ibid.*, nr. 43b.

184   Cf. also Acts 20:36; 21:5.

185   Cf. *Ibid.*, nr. 43c.

186   Cf. *SC*. art. 40; cf. also Congregation for Divine Worship and the Discipline of the Sacraments, *Inst. Varietates Legitimae*, 25 January, 1994, nr. 41: *AAS* 87(1995), p. 304 as quoted in *RGIRM*, nr. 43d.

187   Cf. *RGIRM*, nr. 43d.

188   Cf. *Ibid.*, nr. 43e.

189   Cf. *Ibid.*, nr. 44.

190   Cf. *Ibid.*

191   Cf. Peter Elliot, *Ceremonies of the Modern Roman Rite....*, nr. 22, p. 8.

192   Cf. *SC*. art. 30.

193   RGIRM. Nr. 45.

194   Cf. *Ibid.*

195   Cf. Peter Elliot, *Ceremonies of the Modern Roman Rite...*, nr. 233, p. 87.

196   Cf. RGIRM nr. 82a, p. 40.

197   Cf. *Ibid.*, nr. 82b., p. 40.

198   Cf. Lucien Deiss *The Mass*, The Liturgical Press, Collegeville Minnesota, 1989, p. 92.

199   Cf. Ibid.

## Chapter Seven: Liturgical Homily

200   Cf. *CCC*. nr. 1329.

200   *Dogmatic Constitution On Divine Revelation, Die Verbum*, nr. 21.

201   *Ibid.*, nr. 22.

202   *SC*. nr. 24.

203   Cf. *Ibid.*

204   Cf. Lucien Deiss, *The Mass*, p.41.

205   *SC*. 35:1.

206   Cf. Thanksgiving to Origen, XV, 179, quoted in Lucien Deiss, *The Mass...*, p.42.

207   Cf. *SC*. 41. Cf. also *SC. 42* for the recommended days on which homilies are most suitable, namely, Sundays and holidays of obligation. Others include the week-days of Advent, Lent and Eastertide and on liturgical occasions where there is a large number of people.

208   Cf. . *SC.* 52.

209   Cf. SC. 41and 42. For the recommended days on which homilies are most suitable viz., Sundays and holidays of obligation. Others include the weekdays of Advent, Lent and Eastertide and on liturgical occasions where there is a large number of people.

210   Cf. Sacred Congregation For Divine Worship, *Liturgiae Instaurationes, 5 September, 1970, no. 2ab.*

211   *Acts of the Apostles* 6:2.

212   Cf. Adolf Adam, *The Liturgical Year, Its History and Its Meaning After the Reforms of the Liturgy,* Pueblo Publications Co., New York, 1981, p. 19.

213   Cf. Gabriel M. Braso, *Liturgy and Spirituality*, translated by Leonard J. Doyle, The Liturgical Press, St. John's Abbey, Collegeville, Minnesota, 1971, p. 290.

214   The list was very much limited when it was first given by Rev. Prof. A. Akubue at the priests retreat in the nineties. The author in this book improved on the list and brought it to 35 while the list still remains open to be improved upon by further scholarships.

215   The nature of liturgy demands the use of refined proverbs as some of the local proverbs are obnoxious and unsuitable for a refined assembly as the liturgy. Today incidentally, some of them have been refined such as *Egbe belu ugo belu, nke si ibe ya ebena, gosi ya ebe oga ebe* instead of *nke si ibe ya ebena nku kwapu ya.*

216   Tortoise stories must be told with prudence because of what the animal represents in most of the stories. Often it represents trickery, lies, etc. more harm could be done by telling tortoise stories especially to children indiscriminately. One could end up enthroning the vice of trickery, cheating and lies.

217   Cf. Peter Elliot, *Ceremonies of the Modern Roman Rite,* nr. 209, p. 76.

## Chapter Eight: Practical Questions ...

218   Cf. *SC.* 14.

## General Conclusion

219   *Missale Romanum of Paul VI...*p. 358.

## Appendices

220   Ibid., p. 854.
221   Cf. *Documents on the Sacred Liturgy, (Sacrosanctum Concilium* hence forth SC), nr. 37.
222   *SC.* nrr. 38-39.
223   The acclamations within the Eucharistic prayer are inserted not without reasons. Given the fact that the principal celebrant leads in the Eucharistic prayer, it is also necessary that he be accompanied and supported by the assembly to underscore the active, conscious and full participation of the worshipping community (cf. *SC.* 14).
224   The other alternative responses could equally be used. There are other appropriate responses which could also be used such as: Keep in mind.....; Oh you are Lord...,

# IKO - Verlag für Interkulturelle Kommunikation

## Holger Ehling Publishing • Edition ZeitReise • Edition Hipparchia • Edition ÖKOglobal

### Frankfurt am Main • London

| | | |
|---|---|---|
| **Büro Frankfurt am Main** | Internet: www.iko-verlag.de | **Büro London** |
| Postfach 90 04 21; D-60444 Frankfurt am Main | Verkehrs-Nr.: 10896 | 70 c, Wrentham Avenue |
| Assenheimerstr. 17, D-60489 Frankfurt | VAT-Nr.: DE 111876148 | London NW10 3HG, UK |
| Tel.: +49-(0)69-78 48 08 | Auslieferung: Order@KNO-VA.de | Phone: +44-(0)20-76881688 |
| Fax: +49-(0)69-78 96 575 | | Fax: +44-(0)20-76881699 |
| e-mail: info@iko-verlag.de | | e-mail: HEhling@aol.com |

## Aus dem Verlagsprogramm

Patrick C. Chibuko
**Liturgical Inculturation: An authentic African Response**
2002, 194 S., € 14,80, ISBN 3-88939-636-4

John Chidi Nwafor
**Church and State: The Nigerian Experience**
The relationship between the Church and the State in Nigeria in the areas of Human Rights, Education, Religious Freedom and Religious Tolerance
Ethik – Gesellschaft – Wirtschaft, Band 13
2002, 444 S., € 26,80, ISBN 3-88939-632-1

Missionswissenschaftliches Institut Missio e.V.
**Jahrbuch für kontextuelle Theologien 2002**
Deutsch, Englisch, Spanisch und Französisch
2002, 220 S., € 21,80, ISBN 3-88939-669-0

Norbert Arntz/Raul Fornet-Betancourt/ Georg Wolter (Hrsg.)
**Werkstatt „Reich Gottes"**
Befreiungstheologische Impulse in der Praxis
2002, 352 S , € 35,80, ISBN 3-88939- 638-0

Franz Josef Stendebach
**Wege der Menschen**
Versuche zu einer Anthropologie des Alten Testaments
Ethik – Gesellschaft – Wirtschaft, Band 11
2001, 348 S., € 21,80, ISBN 3-88939-558-9

Paulo Suess
**Weltweit artikuliert, kontextuell verwurzelt**
Theologie und Kirche Lateinamerikas vor den Herausforderungen des ‚dritten Subjekts'
Zeugnisse, Analysen, Perspektiven
Theologie Interkulturell, Band 12
2001, 276 S., € 22,80, ISBN 3-88939-623-2

Christian Hellmann
**Religiöse Bildung, Interreligiöses Lernen und Interkulturelle Pädagogik**
Eine religionsgeschichtliche Untersuchung zur religiösen und interkulturellen Erziehung in der Moderne
2001, 344 S., € 29,80, ISBN 3-88939-571-6

Raúl Fornet-Betancourt (Hrsg.)
**Kapitalistische Globalisierung und Befreiung**
Religiöse Erfahrungen und Option für das Leben
Denktraditionen im Dialog, Band 9
2000, 506 S., € 39,80, ISBN 3-88939-543-0

Raúl Fornet-Betancourt (Hrsg.)
**Theologie im III. Millennium – Quo vadis?**
Antworten der Theologen. Dokumentation einer Weltumfrage
Beiträge in Deutsch, Englisch, Spanisch und Französisch
Denktraditionen im Dialog, Band 7
2000, 310 S., € 24,00, ISBN 3-88939-517-1

**Bestellen Sie bitte über den Buchhandel oder direkt beim Verlag.
Wir senden Ihnen gerne unser Titelverzeichnis zu.**